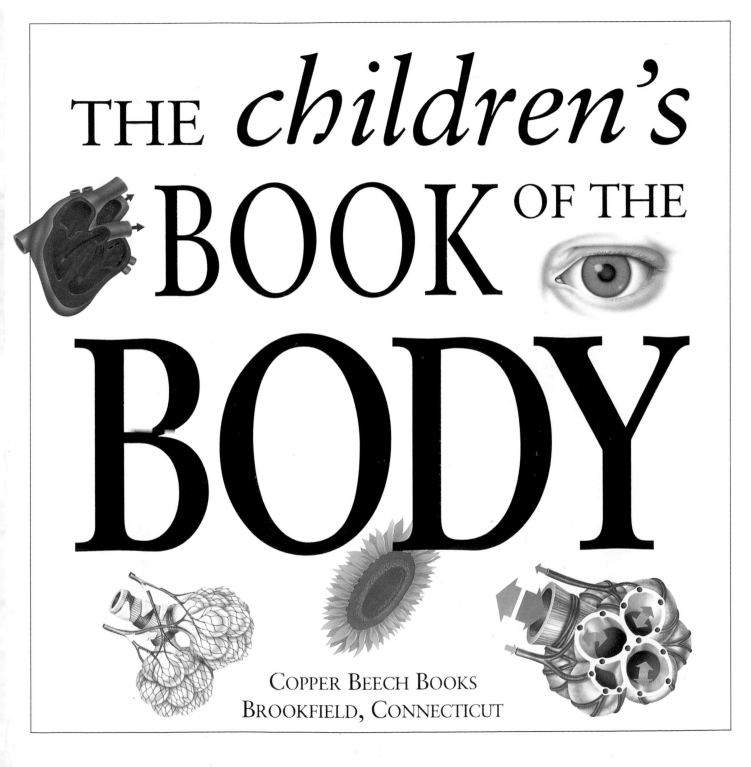

THE *children's* BOOK OF THE BODY

COPPER BEECH BOOKS
BROOKFIELD, CONNECTICUT

Contents

Chapter One
Skin and Hair 4

Chapter Two
Bones 18

Chapter Three
Blood 36

Chapter Four
Breathing 54

Chapter Five
Eating 70

Chapter Six
Senses 88

Chapter Seven
Brain 104

Did you know? 122

Glossary 124

Index 126

This edition produced in 1996 for
Copper Beech Books,
an imprint of The Millbrook Press
2 Old New Milford Road
Brookfield
Connecticut 06804
© Aladdin Books Ltd 1996
28 Percy Street
London W1P 0LD
Produced by Aladdin Books Ltd
All rights reserved
Printed in Italy

Library of Congress Cataloging-in-Publication Data
Sandeman, Anna.
The children's book of the body/by Anna Sandeman; illustrated by Ian Thompson.
p. cm. Includes index
Summary: Shows how the inside of the body looks with explanations of how different
systems and body parts work.
ISBN 0-7613-0519-X (hc)
1. Human physiology – – Juvenile literature. 2. Human anatomy – – Juvenile literature.
[1. Body, human.] I. Thompson, Ian, 1964– ill. II. Title.
QP37.S25 1996
612–dc20   96-13909
                                                    CIP AC

The Human Body

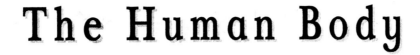

Have you ever wondered what happens inside your body? Every day you eat, sleep, breathe, move about, see, taste, and feel, most of the time without being aware of it happening. So just how is your body able to do all of these amazing things? This book will literally get under your skin to reveal the workings of the inner self and show you the answer to some very important questions:

What makes your heart beat quicker?

Why does your tummy rumble?

What happens if you break a bone?

And many more...

Chapter One
Skin and Hair

Your skin   6

The epidermis   8

The dermis   10

Hair   12

How hair grows   14

Types of hair   16

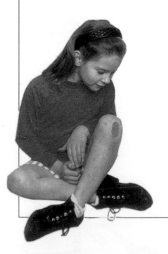

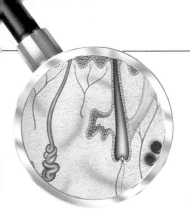

Introduction

Your body is surrounded by a flexible
and protective covering – skin. This
shield protects you from dirt,
microscopic animals, and injuries.

Covering most of this protective case is a coat
of hair, which is thicker in parts, such as on
your head. This layer of hair keeps you warm.

Together, skin and hair form the first
layer of defense against the perils of
the outside world.

Your skin

Your skin is the largest single part of you. If it were laid out flat, it would cover a space of about 16 square feet (1.5 sq meters), the area of a twin bedsheet.

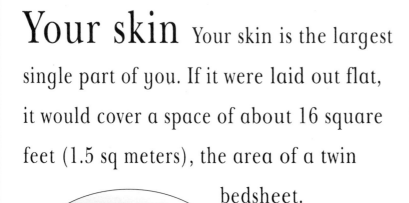

Most of your skin is about 0.08 inch (2 millimeters) thick. But on your eyelids, it is less than 0.04 inch (1 millimeter) thick. The skin on the palms of your hands and the soles of your feet is up to 0.2 inch (4.5 millimeters) thick. It is thicker here because it has to stand up to heavy use.

When you are young, your skin fits you snugly. Unlike a snake, which has to shed its skin from time to time, you have skin which grows with you. After the age of 25 or so, your skin becomes less elastic. Wrinkles and creases appear as you get older and your skin becomes looser.

The color of your skin stays more or less the same throughout your life. Its shade depends on how much melanin it has. Melanin is a type of coloring which protects skin from the sun's harmful rays. People from hotter countries usually have more melanin than those in cooler places, and so their skin is darker.

The epidermis

Everybody's skin is made up of two main layers – the epidermis on top, and the dermis below. As in all parts of the body, the skin is made up of tiny cells. New skin cells are formed at the bottom of the epidermis. They move upward until the older cells above are forced to the skin's surface. This takes about three weeks. During this time, the older cells die. They are squeezed and flattened together to form a tough outer layer which covers the whole body.

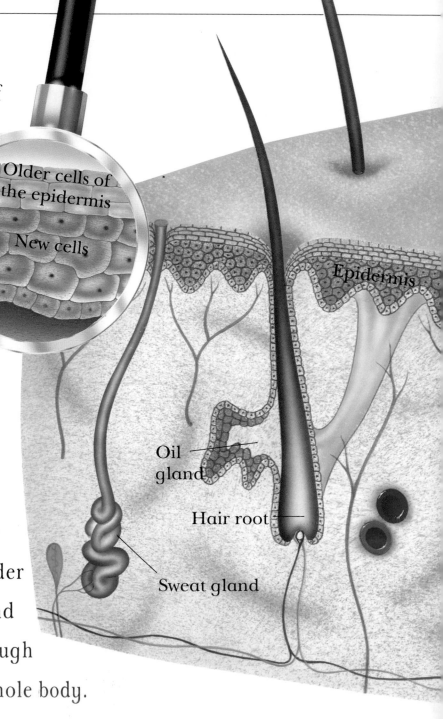

Older cells of the epidermis

New cells

Epidermis

Oil gland

Hair root

Sweat gland

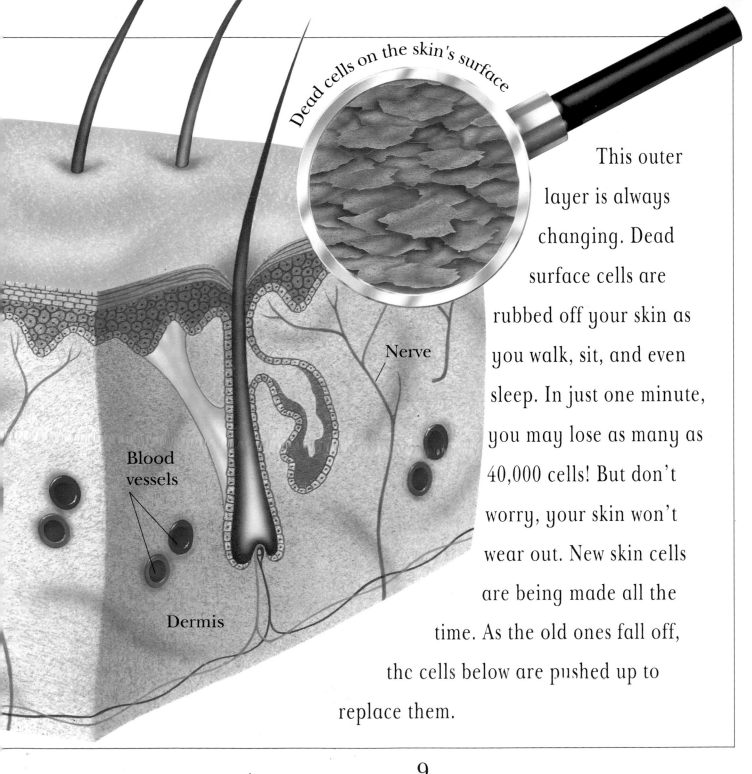

Dead cells on the skin's surface

Nerve

Blood vessels

Dermis

This outer layer is always changing. Dead surface cells are rubbed off your skin as you walk, sit, and even sleep. In just one minute, you may lose as many as 40,000 cells! But don't worry, your skin won't wear out. New skin cells are being made all the time. As the old ones fall off, the cells below are pushed up to replace them.

How hair grows

Every hair grows from its root in the dermis layer of the skin. The root is inside a kind of tiny tube of skin, called a follicle.

Cells grow together at the bottom of each follicle to make a tough material called keratin. As keratin forms, the hair grows up from the root and out of the follicle. The cells die as they reach the skin's surface. Only the root of the hair is alive, the part you see is dead.

Even the hair on your head is dead. The reason it looks shiny and healthy is because each hair has its own oil gland at its root.

Close-up of a hair

14

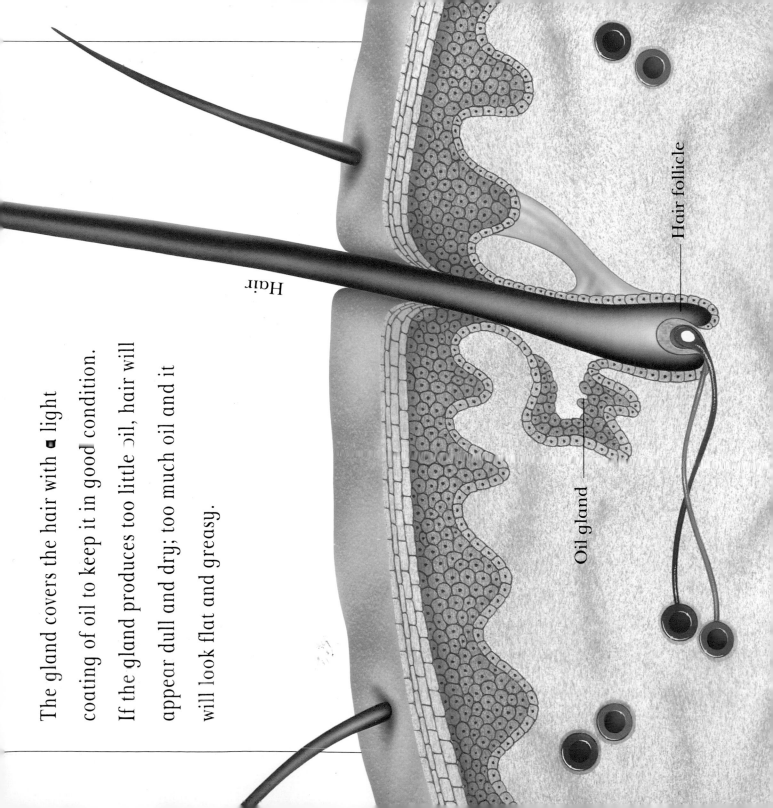

The gland covers the hair with a light coating of oil to keep it in good condition. If the gland produces too little oil, hair will appear dull and dry; too much oil and it will look flat and greasy.

Hair

Hair follicle

Oil gland

Types of hair

The type of hair you have depends on the size and shape of your hair follicles. If you have large follicles, your hair will be thick and heavy; if you have narrow follicles, it will be fine and flyaway.

The shape of your follicles decides how straight or curly your hair will be. Straight hair grows from round follicles. Oval follicles force hairs to bend and become wavy. Flat follicles coil hairs into curls.

Round follicle

Oval follicle

Flat follicle

16

Your hair color is probably like that of your parents or grandparents. It may be black, brown, red, blond – or any shade between. Your skin color also affects the color of your hair.

Make a chart showing what color of hair each of your friends has. Which is the most common color of hair?

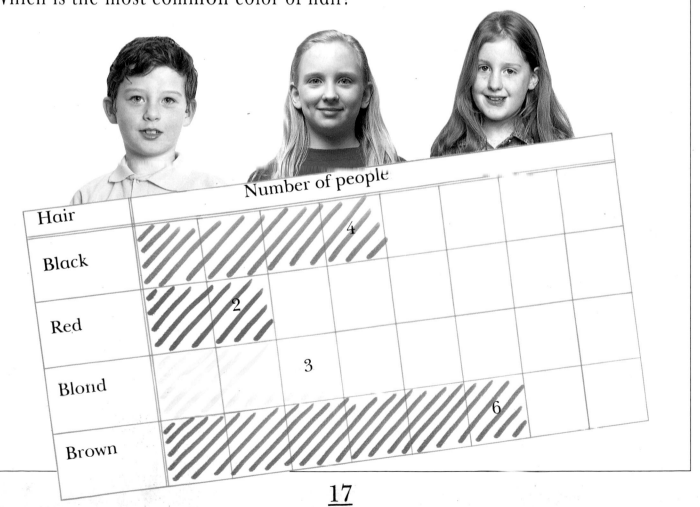

Hair	Number of people						
Black				4			
Red		2					
Blond			3				
Brown						6	

What are bones?

Some people think bones are just brittle, dried-up, sticklike things. In fact, living bones are just as much alive as the rest of you. Throughout your life they keep growing and changing shape to give your body the support it needs.

This skeleton is over 1,000 years old. Your bones are very different from these.

What would you look like without any bones?

Bones are made up of different parts.

Marrow

Compact bone

The outer part of the bone is smooth and hard. This is called compact bone. The inner part looks more like a sponge, and is called spongy bone.

Spongy bone

Spongy bone is lighter than compact bone, but still hard and strong.

Inside many bones is a fatty jelly called bone marrow. This is where most of your blood cells are made.

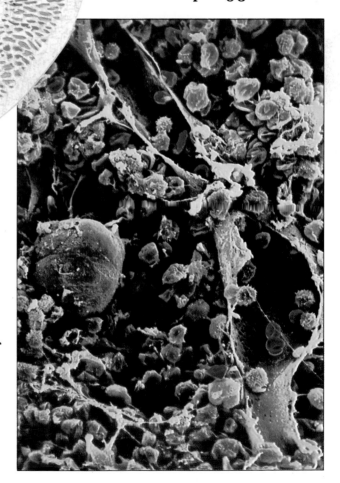

You can see the blood cells in this magnified picture of bone marrow.

The human skeleton

When you were born, you had over 300 bones. They were very soft. They were made of a kind of gristle, called cartilage, as well as firmer bone. As you began to develop, the cartilage hardened into bone and some bones grew together. This will go on happening until you become a fully-grown adult. By that time you will have just over 200 bones, although you will be more than three times the height you were at birth!

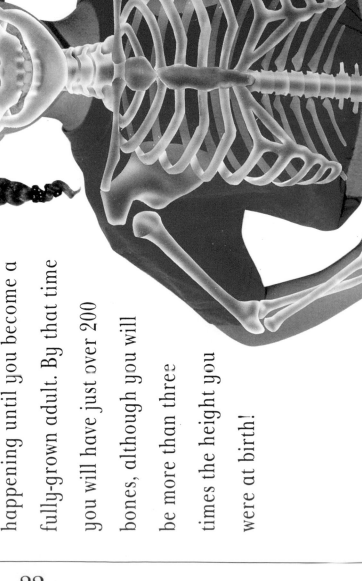

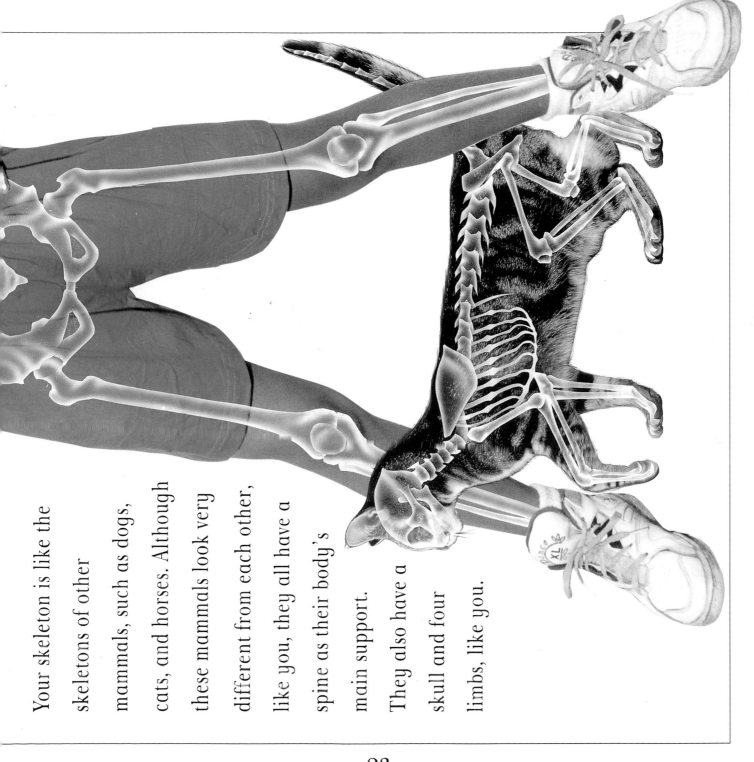

Your skeleton is like the skeletons of other mammals, such as dogs, cats, and horses. Although these mammals look very different from each other, like you, they all have a spine as their body's main support. They also have a skull and four limbs, like you.

Fingers, hands, and arms

Write your name. It's easy isn't it? But only because your hand is made so cleverly! Each hand has 27 bones with three in each finger, and two in each thumb. These bones allow your hand to curve around your pen. Now try writing your name keeping your fingers and thumb straight.

Paint a picture in the air. Watch your hand move up and down at your wrist. Now keep your arm straight and draw a circle in the air. You can do this because the eight bones in your wrist allow you to move your hand almost any way you want.

28

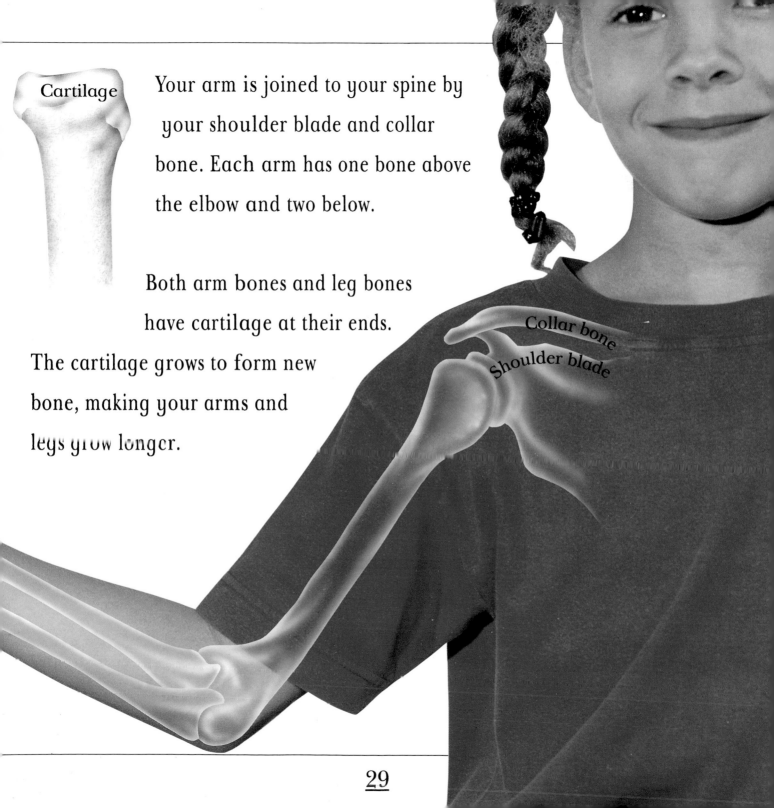

Cartilage

Your arm is joined to your spine by your shoulder blade and collar bone. Each arm has one bone above the elbow and two below.

Both arm bones and leg bones have cartilage at their ends. The cartilage grows to form new bone, making your arms and legs grow longer.

Collar bone

Shoulder blade

Joints

The place where two bones meet is called a joint. There are fixed joints and moving joints. Fixed joints, such as those in the skull, do not move. Moving joints allow you to bend, twist, or turn different parts of your body.

There are two main types of moving joint. Your elbows and knees have hinge joints. They allow your arms and legs to bend and straighten. These joints move in one direction only, like a door hinge.

Hinge joint

Hinge joints are also found between the bones in your fingers and toes.

Joints which can move in any direction are called ball-and-socket joints. These are at your shoulders and hips. Here the rounded end of one bone is held inside a cup-shaped hollow in the other.

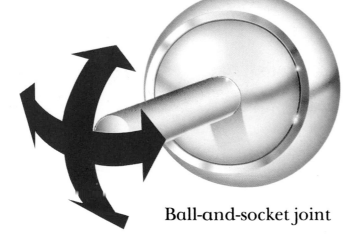

Ball-and-socket joint

All joints are coated with a special fluid, which acts like oil, to help them move. The bones are held in place by strong straps, like rubber bands, called ligaments.

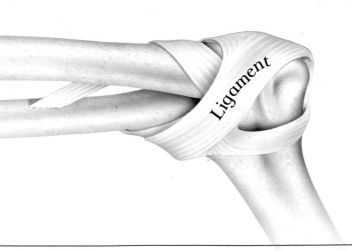

Ligament

Broken bones

Although a healthy bone is very strong, it can still break. If you hit a bone very hard, or bend a joint too far the wrong way, the bone will snap.

Greenstick fracture

There are different kinds of breaks, or fractures. A greenstick fracture is the least serious because only part of the bone breaks. In a simple fracture, the bone breaks cleanly in two. In a compound fracture, the bone breaks so that part of it pokes through the skin.

Simple fracture

Have you ever broken a bone? Make a chart to show how many of your friends have broken bones. Which ones have they broken? How long did the bones take to heal?

Compound fracture

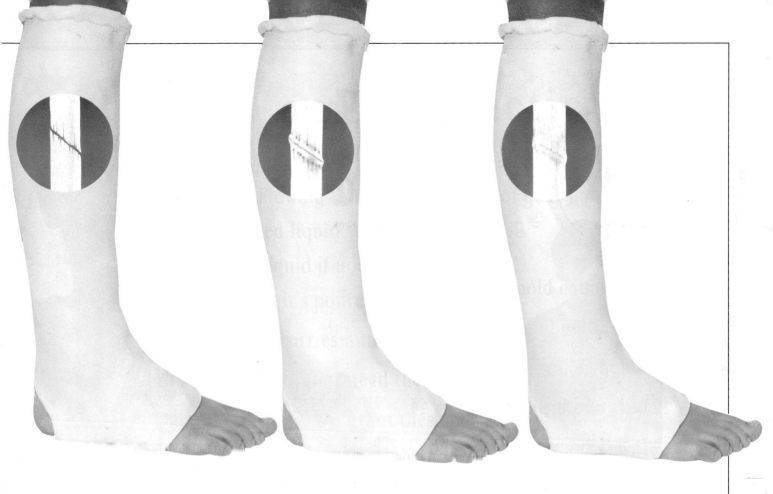

All broken bones mend themselves in the same way. First a blood clot forms to close up the space between the broken ends. The bone cells begin to grow on each side of the break. The cells gradually close the gap with new bone. A plaster cast keeps the pieces in place. It usually takes about twelve weeks for a broken bone to heal.

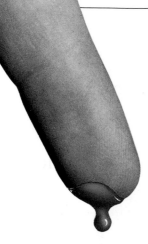

How much blood?

Ouch! You have cut yourself. Blood oozes out of the wound and trickles down your finger. It is bright red. It feels warm and slightly sticky.

If you cut yourself the cut should be cleaned and covered up to stop any germs from getting in. If the cut is small it will heal quickly.

If the cut is very deep then you may need some stitches to hold the cut together until it heals.

When you cut yourself it may feel as if you are losing a lot of blood. But don't worry, you have plenty left. A three-year-old has two pints or more of blood in his or her body – enough to fill a large milk carton; a grown-up has five times this amount. Your body won't notice if it has a few drops less for awhile. In fact, you could lose up to a third of your blood and still survive.

What blood does

Your blood travels around your body like a fast-flowing river.

The blood flowing through your body is known as your bloodstream. It carries the supplies your body needs to grow and stay healthy.

Blood also takes away waste and helps your body to fight off disease and heal wounds.

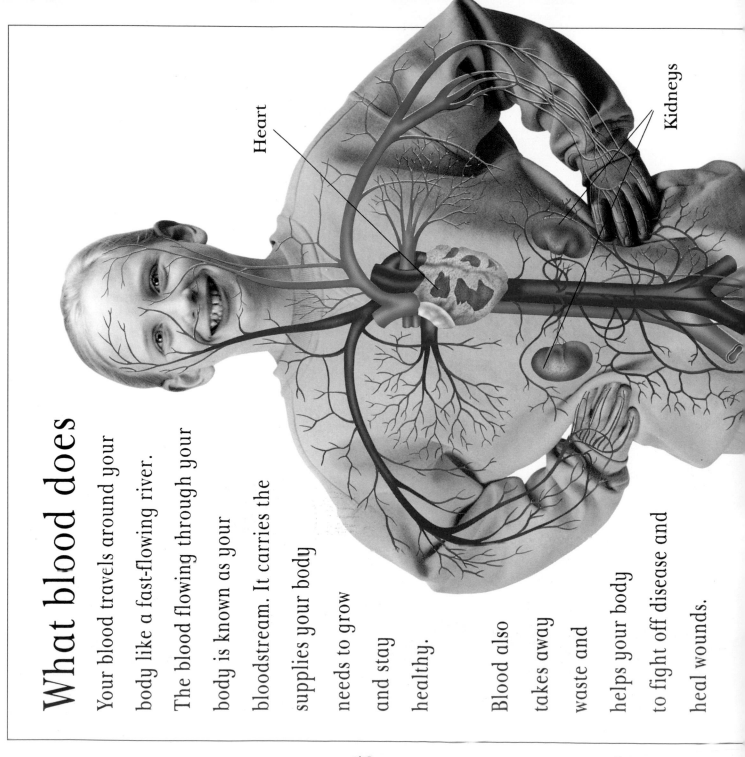

Heart

Kidneys

Most of your blood is made up of a yellowish liquid called plasma. It takes the nutrients from the food you eat to all parts of your body.

Plasma also takes waste to your kidneys. Your kidneys then filter your blood to take out any waste. You get rid of the waste when you go to the bathroom.

The purified blood goes back into your bloodstream to continue its journey around your body.

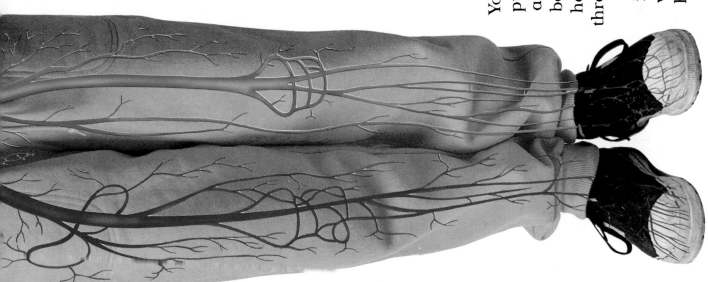

Your blood is pumped around your body by the heart. It travels through arteries (shown here in red) and veins (shown here in blue).

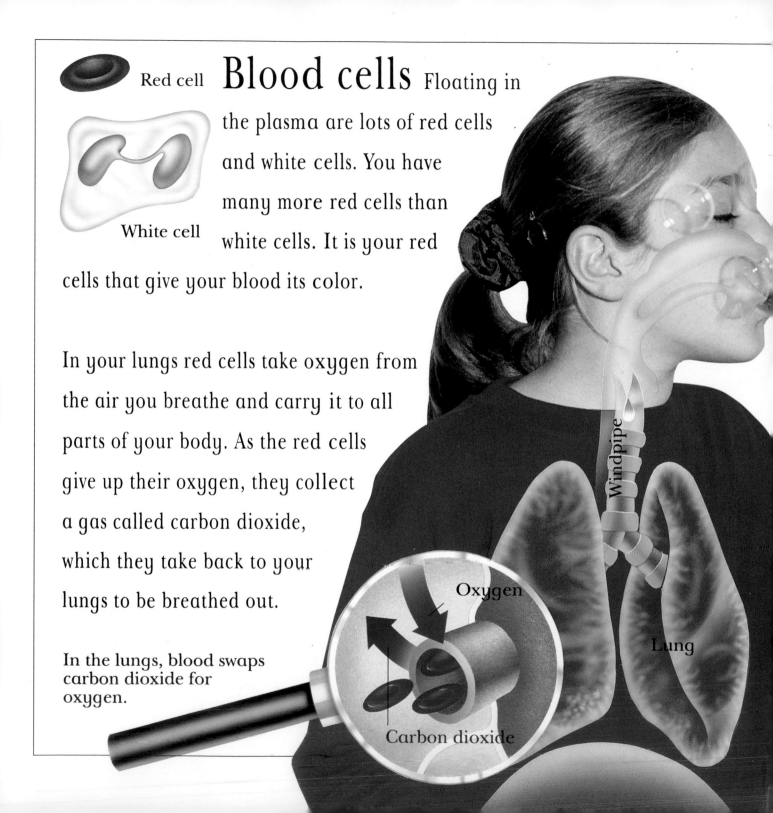

Red cell

White cell

Blood cells
Floating in the plasma are lots of red cells and white cells. You have many more red cells than white cells. It is your red cells that give your blood its color.

In your lungs red cells take oxygen from the air you breathe and carry it to all parts of your body. As the red cells give up their oxygen, they collect a gas called carbon dioxide, which they take back to your lungs to be breathed out.

In the lungs, blood swaps carbon dioxide for oxygen.

Oxygen

Carbon dioxide

Windpipe

Lung

White cells are much bigger than red cells. Their job is to kill any germs that get into your body. Some germs are so strong they can kill white cells. If your body is attacked by lots of germs, it makes extra white cells to fight them off.

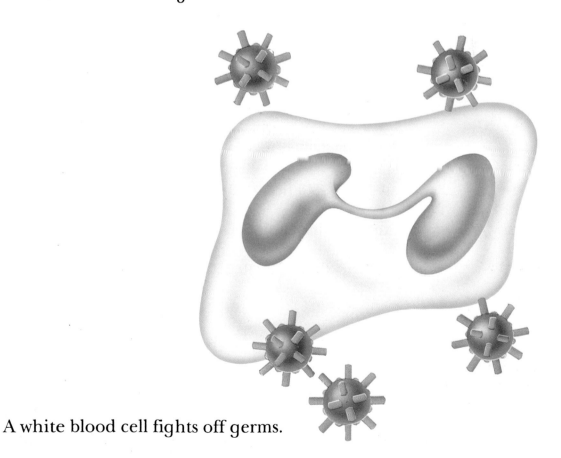

A white blood cell fights off germs.

Cuts and bruises

When you cut yourself, blood flows out quickly at first. But unless the cut is very deep, it soon stops.

Special repair cells in your blood make a kind of glue, which sticks together tiny drops of blood to form a clot.

The clot acts like a plug to stop any more blood from leaking out. It also stops any germs from getting in. The clot then dries into a scab, which falls off once new skin has grown underneath.

When did you last get a bruise?
How did it happen?

If you bump yourself
hard you get a bruise.
A bruise is formed
because the blood leaks
into your skin and
makes a black-and-blue
mark on the surface.
After a few days the
bruise turns yellow. The
leaked blood is gradually
broken down in the skin
and the bruise
fades away.

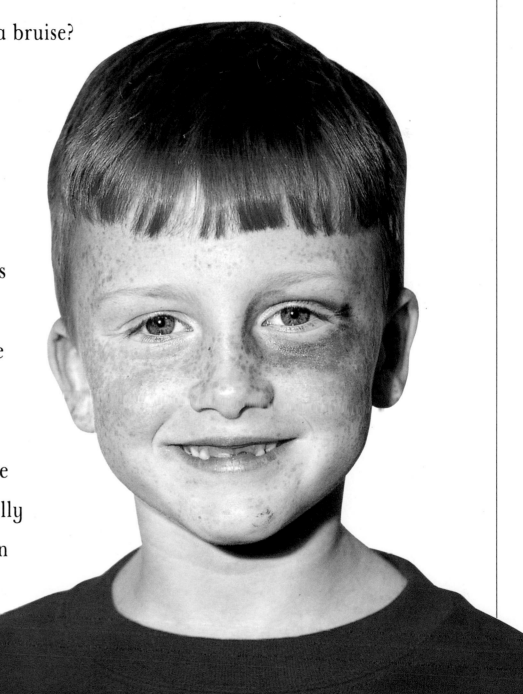

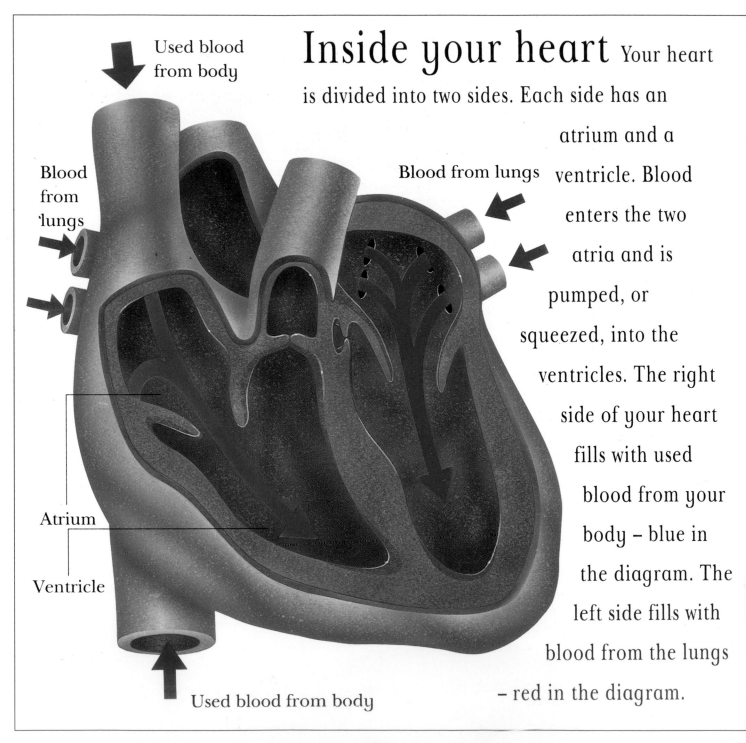

Used blood from body

Blood from lungs

Blood from lungs

Blood from lungs

Inside your heart
Your heart is divided into two sides. Each side has an atrium and a ventricle. Blood enters the two atria and is pumped, or squeezed, into the ventricles. The right side of your heart fills with used blood from your body – blue in the diagram. The left side fills with blood from the lungs – red in the diagram.

Atrium

Ventricle

Used blood from body

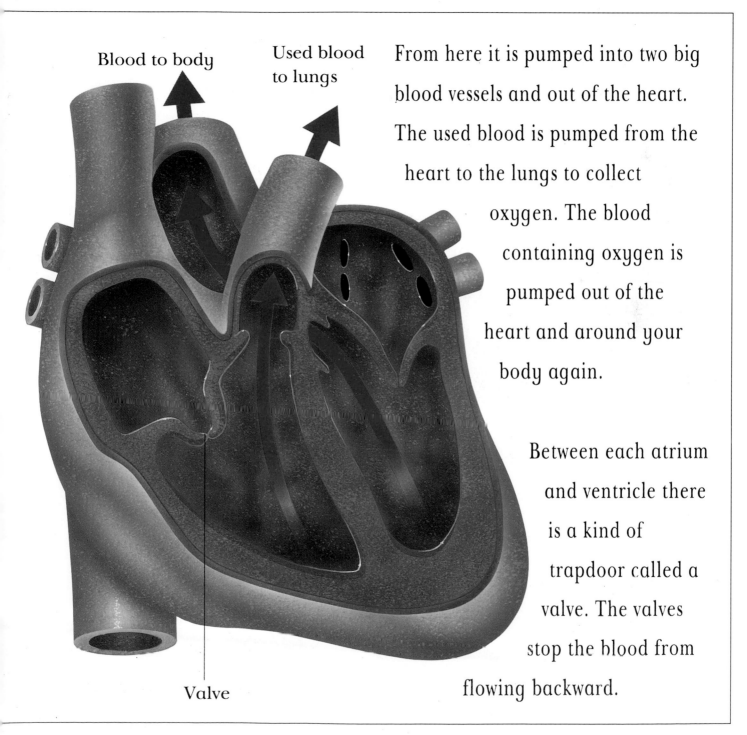

Blood to body

Used blood to lungs

Valve

From here it is pumped into two big blood vessels and out of the heart. The used blood is pumped from the heart to the lungs to collect oxygen. The blood containing oxygen is pumped out of the heart and around your body again.

Between each atrium and ventricle there is a kind of trapdoor called a valve. The valves stop the blood from flowing backward.

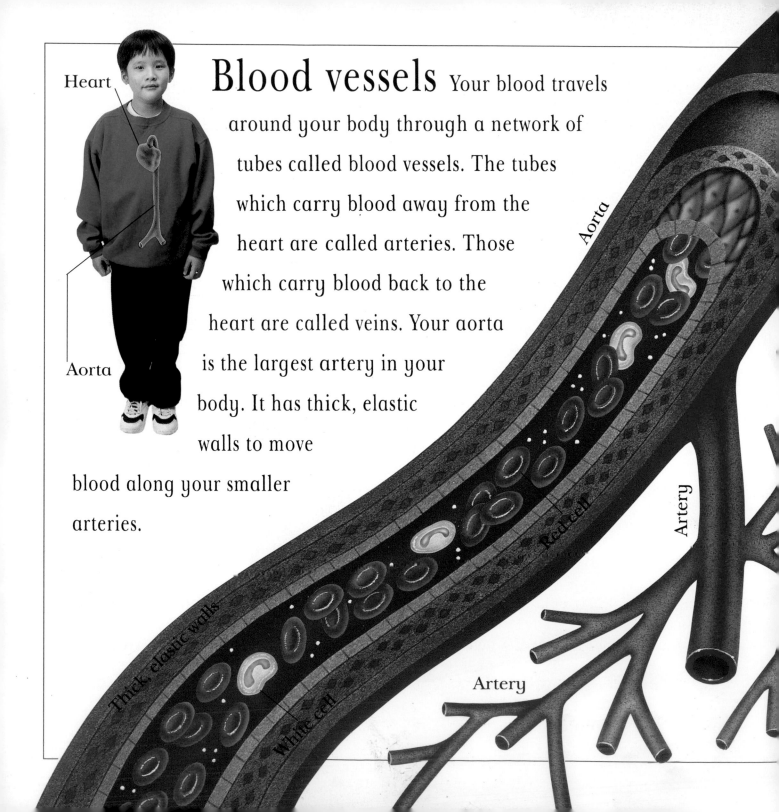

Heart

Aorta

Blood vessels Your blood travels around your body through a network of tubes called blood vessels. The tubes which carry blood away from the heart are called arteries. Those which carry blood back to the heart are called veins. Your aorta is the largest artery in your body. It has thick, elastic walls to move blood along your smaller arteries.

Aorta

Aorta

Artery

Red cell

Thick, elastic walls

White cell

Artery

Your arteries split into smaller and smaller tubes to reach every part of your body. The smallest tubes are called capillaries. These are just wide enough for one red blood cell to pass through at a time. Look closely at your eye. The red lines you can see are capillaries.

Have you noticed that your face often gets red after you have run a race or played an energetic game? Do you know why this happens?

When you are very hot, your capillaries widen so that more blood can reach the surface of your skin to cool down.

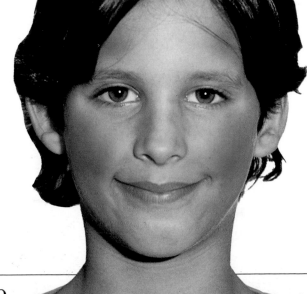

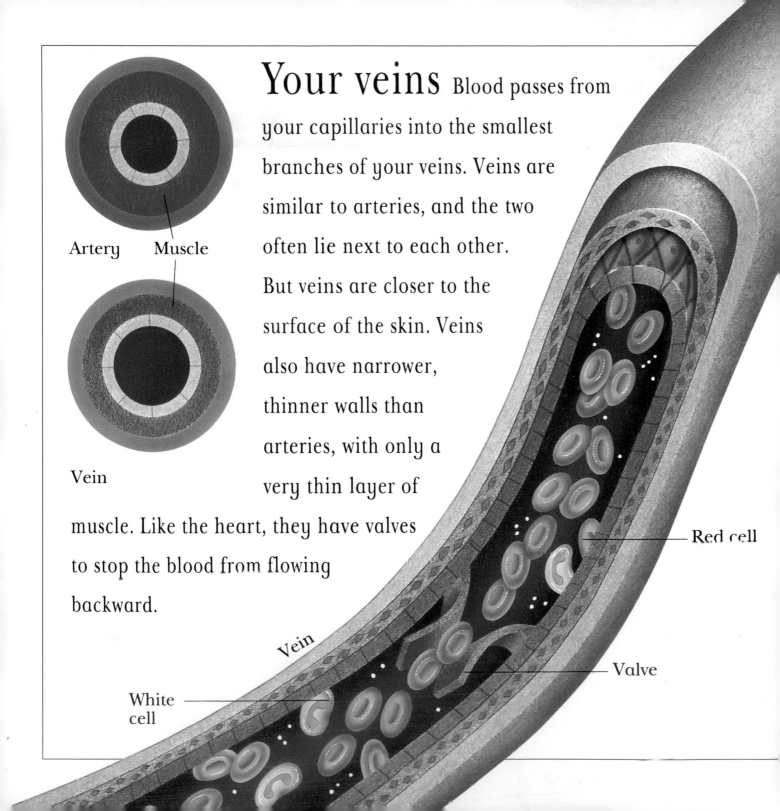

Your veins

Blood passes from your capillaries into the smallest branches of your veins. Veins are similar to arteries, and the two often lie next to each other. But veins are closer to the surface of the skin. Veins also have narrower, thinner walls than arteries, with only a very thin layer of muscle. Like the heart, they have valves to stop the blood from flowing backward.

Artery

Muscle

Vein

Vein

White cell

Red cell

Valve

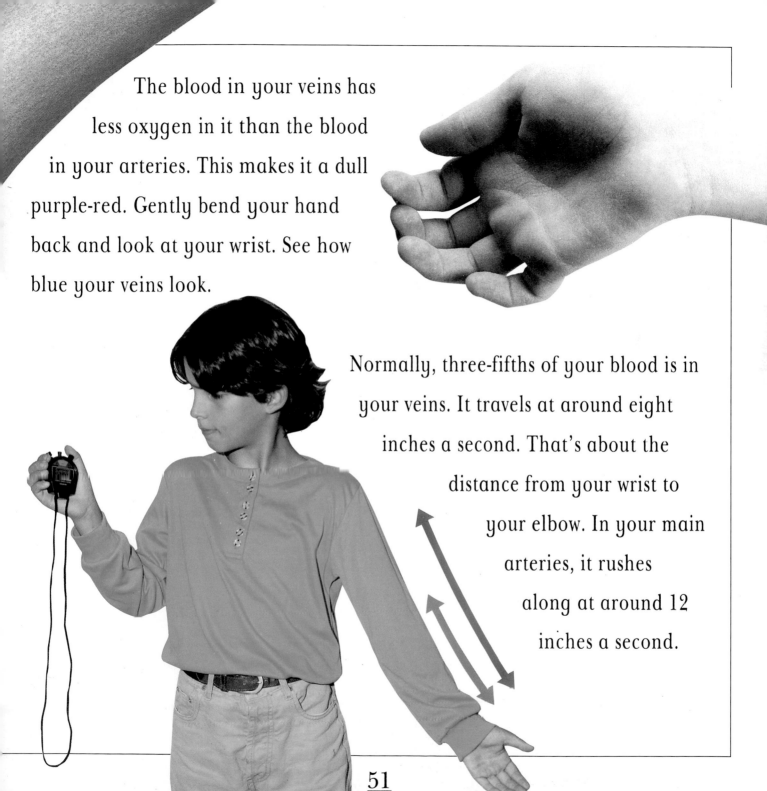

The blood in your veins has less oxygen in it than the blood in your arteries. This makes it a dull purple-red. Gently bend your hand back and look at your wrist. See how blue your veins look.

Normally, three-fifths of your blood is in your veins. It travels at around eight inches a second. That's about the distance from your wrist to your elbow. In your main arteries, it rushes along at around 12 inches a second.

Your heart rate

The number of times your heart beats in one minute is called your heart rate. If you use up a lot of energy, your brain sends a message to your heart, telling it to pump more blood to your muscles. Your heart rate speeds up, and so does your pulse.

If your muscles need it, they can demand over four-fifths of your blood. Usually, they work well on only one fifth.

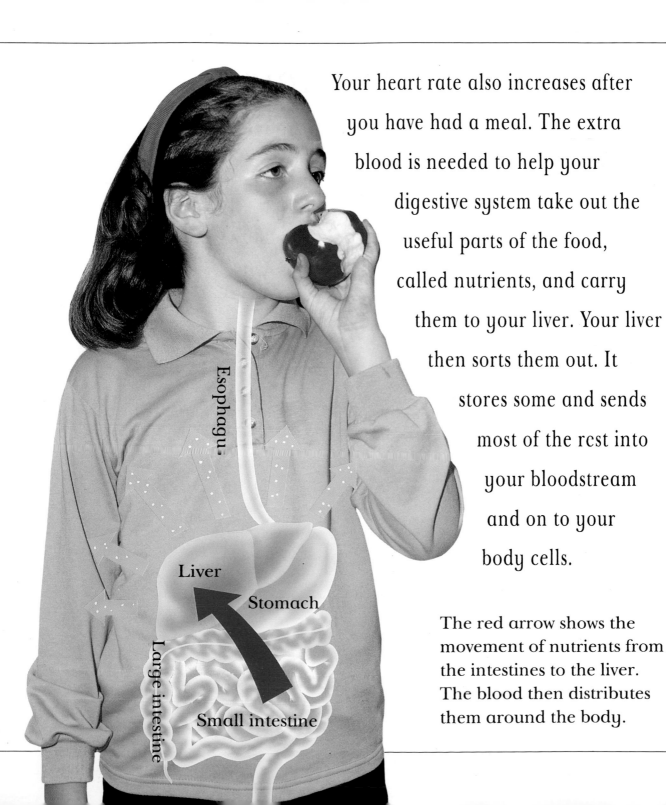

Your heart rate also increases after you have had a meal. The extra blood is needed to help your digestive system take out the useful parts of the food, called nutrients, and carry them to your liver. Your liver then sorts them out. It stores some and sends most of the rest into your bloodstream and on to your body cells.

Esophagus

Liver

Stomach

Large intestine

Small intestine

The red arrow shows the movement of nutrients from the intestines to the liver. The blood then distributes them around the body.

Chapter Four
Breathing

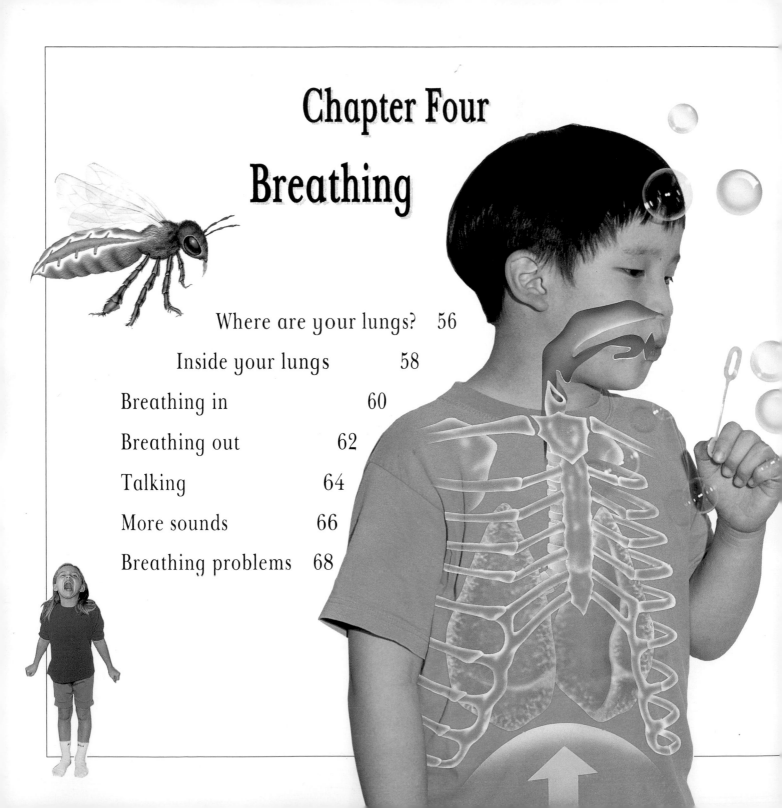

Where are your lungs?   56

Inside your lungs   58

Breathing in   60

Breathing out   62

Talking   64

More sounds   66

Breathing problems   68

Introduction

Without realizing it most of the time, you are continuously breathing, inflating and deflating the organs inside your chest. These are called lungs.

Each time you take a breath you take oxygen into your inflated lungs. Without this vital gas you would suffocate and die.

Breathing out then lets you get rid of unwanted things, such as carbon dioxide, as well as helping you to talk.

Where are your lungs?

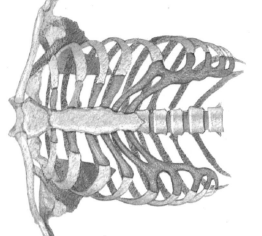

You have two lungs, one on each side of your chest. The left lung is smaller than the right to leave room for your heart! If you could touch your lungs, they would feel soft and spongy.

Just below your lungs is a large sheet of muscle called the diaphragm. This is a kind of wall between your lungs and the rest of your trunk. Like your rib muscles, your diaphragm tightens and relaxes as you breathe in and out.

Your lungs are found inside your rib cage. This is formed by twelve pairs of ribs, ten of which curve around from your backbone to meet up at the front. Muscles between your ribs tighten and relax to allow your rib cage to move.

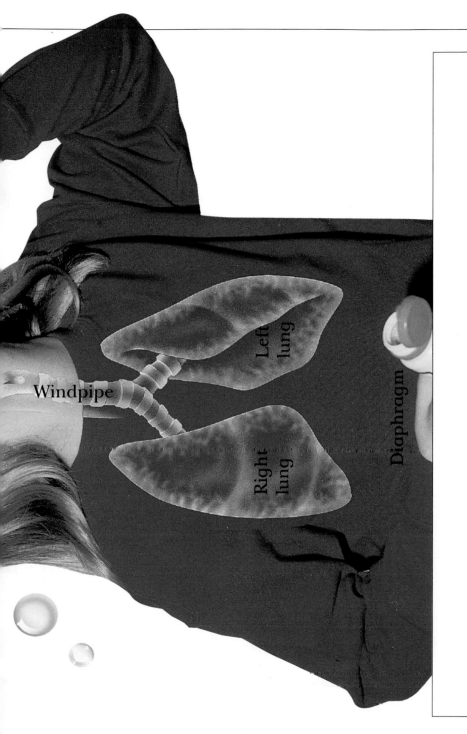

Windpipe

Left lung

Right lung

Diaphragm

Next time you get undressed, look in the mirror and raise your arms above your head. You will see the outline of your rib cage quite clearly.

Inside your lungs

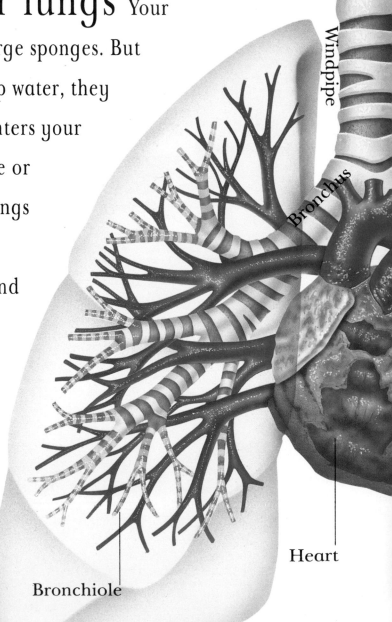

Your lungs are like two large sponges. But instead of soaking up water, they fill up with air. Air enters your body through your nose or mouth. It reaches your lungs through two tubes called bronchi, which fork left and right off your windpipe.

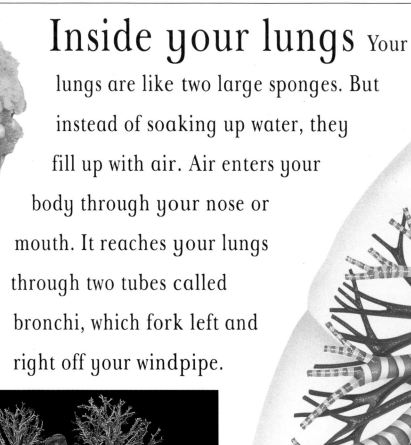

Windpipe

Bronchus

Bronchiole

Heart

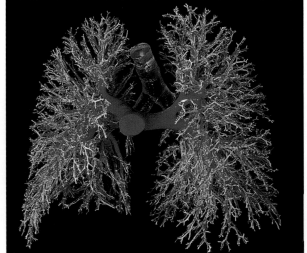

This model shows the bronchi and bronchioles in a pair of lungs.

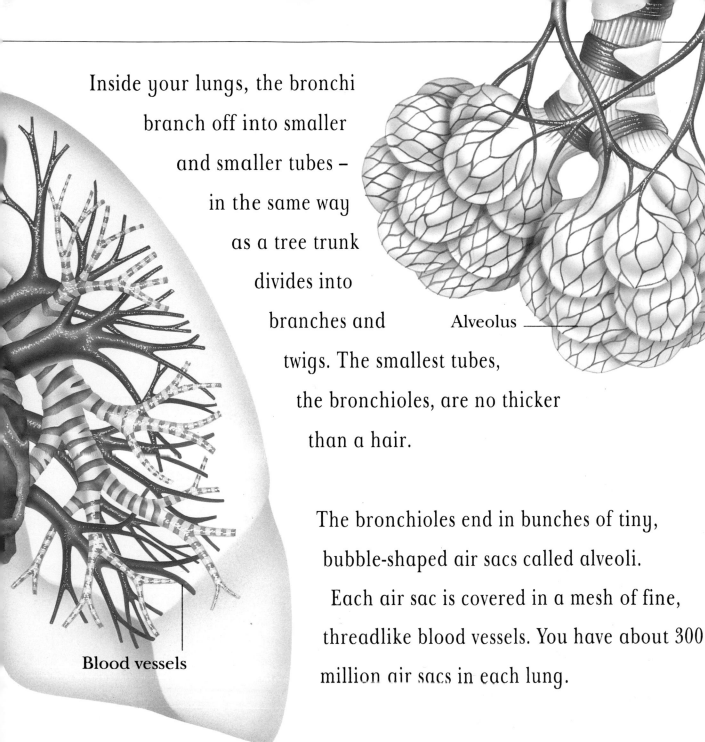

Inside your lungs, the bronchi branch off into smaller and smaller tubes – in the same way as a tree trunk divides into branches and twigs. The smallest tubes, the bronchioles, are no thicker than a hair.

Alveolus

The bronchioles end in bunches of tiny, bubble-shaped air sacs called alveoli. Each air sac is covered in a mesh of fine, threadlike blood vessels. You have about 300 million air sacs in each lung.

Blood vessels

Breathing in

When you need to take a breath, your diaphragm tightens and moves down. Your rib muscles also tighten, forcing your ribs to move up and out. There is now more space in your chest, and air rushes in to fill it.

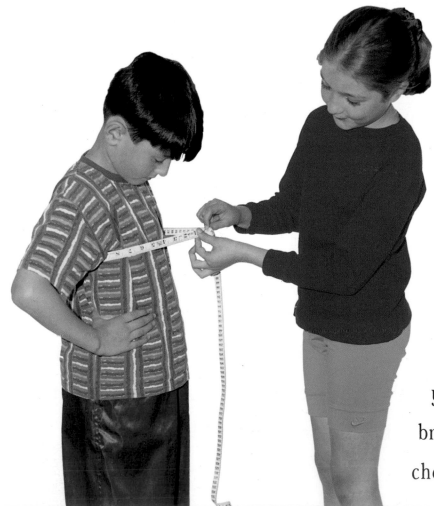

Put your hand on your chest. You can feel your ribs move with each breath.

Breathe out as far as you can. Ask a friend to measure your chest. Next take a deep breath in. How big is your chest now?

Air is sucked into your nose or mouth, down your throat, and into your windpipe. From here it goes through the bronchi and the bronchioles, and into the air sacs. The air sacs fill up with air and your lungs expand.

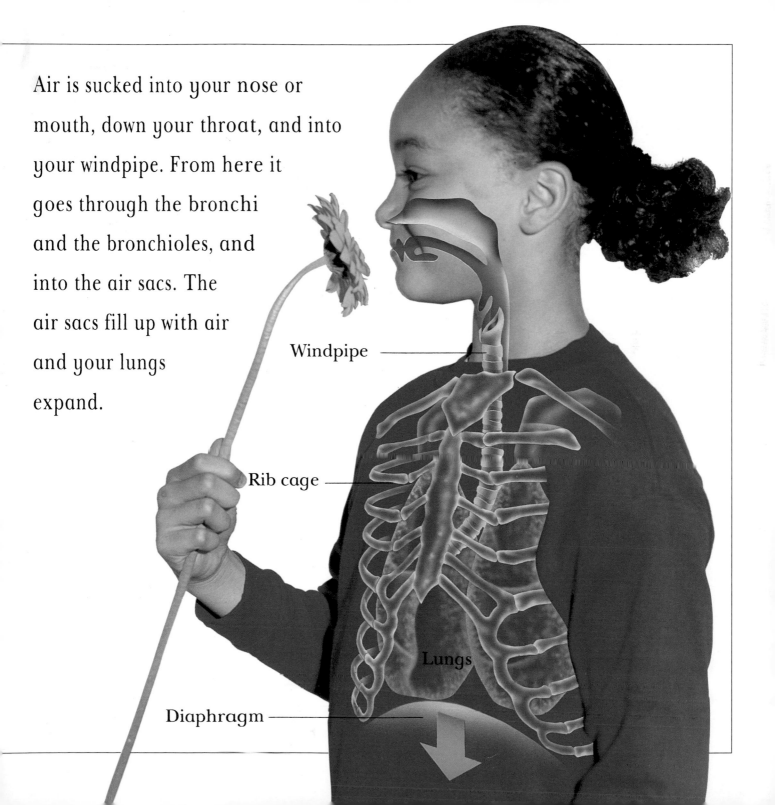

Windpipe

Rib cage

Lungs

Diaphragm

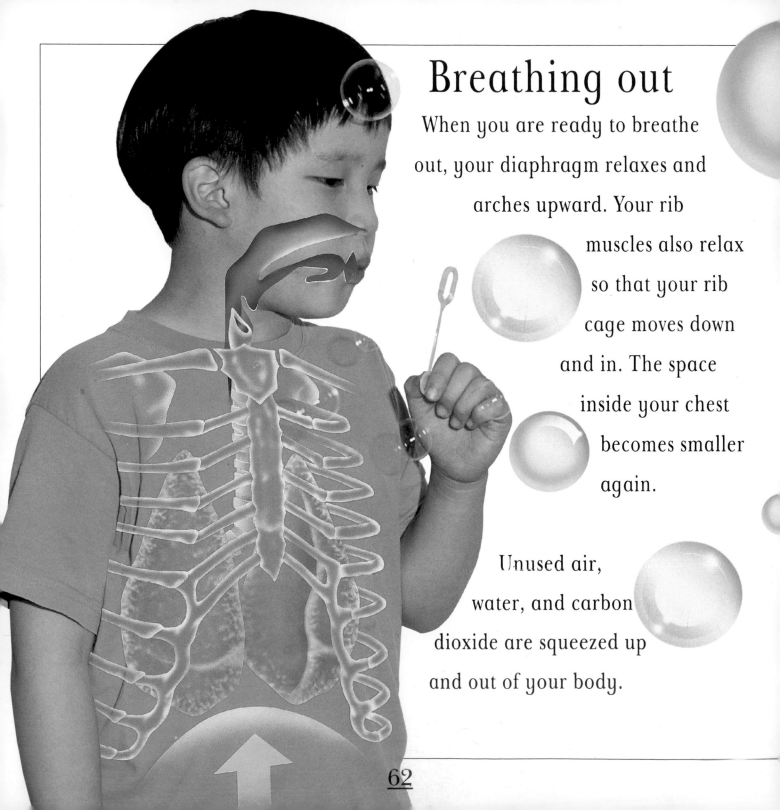

Breathing out

When you are ready to breathe out, your diaphragm relaxes and arches upward. Your rib muscles also relax so that your rib cage moves down and in. The space inside your chest becomes smaller again.

Unused air, water, and carbon dioxide are squeezed up and out of your body.

Air that you breathe out carries heat from the warm inner parts of your body. You can feel how warm it is if you cup your hands over your mouth as you breathe out.

See for yourself the water that is in the air you breathe out. Put a small mirror in the refrigerator for about an hour. Wipe it and hold it in front of your mouth as you breathe out. The water in your breath becomes a fog of droplets on the cold mirror.

Talking

Breathing is also used for talking. As you breathe out, air is pushed up your windpipe and into your voice box. Can you feel your adam's apple? Your voice box is just behind it.

Across the opening to your voice box are two pearly-pink ridges. These are your vocal cords. When air flows between the cords, they vibrate and make sounds.

You can stretch or loosen the cords to make higher or lower sounds.

Adam's apple

The different positions of your tongue, teeth, cheeks, and lips form the sounds into words.

The harder you breathe out, the louder the sounds. Take a deep breath. See how long you can whisper without taking another breath. Now try again – this time shouting. Because you use more breath to shout, you cannot keep going so long.

More sounds

You can make other sounds while breathing. You laugh by taking a deep breath in, then letting it out in a rat-tat-tat of short breaths. You cry in the same way. A yawn is an extra-deep breath in, a sigh is a long breath out.

Sneezes and coughs are noisy blasts of air that help get rid of dirt or mucus in your nose or air tubes. A sneeze can explode at a speed of more than 100 miles (160 kilometers) an hour!

Mucus is a sticky liquid which traps specks of dust and dirt. Tiny hairs in your air tubes, called cilia, gently sweep the mucus away from the lungs up to your nose or mouth to be sneezed or coughed out. A cough can also blow out food which has gone down the wrong way.

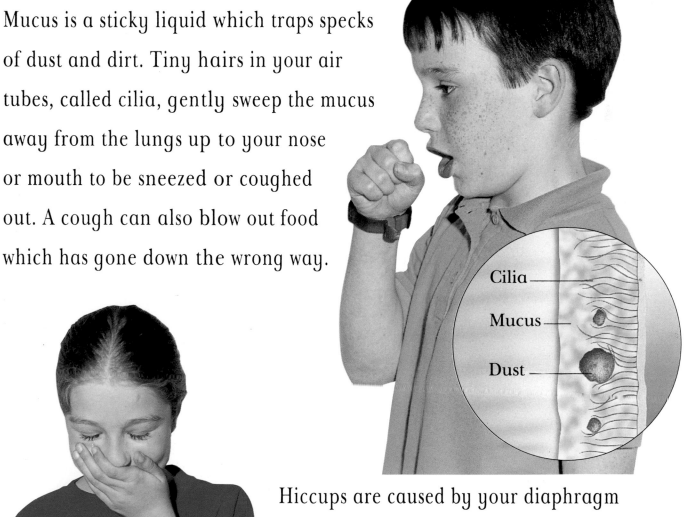

Cilia

Mucus

Dust

Hiccups are caused by your diaphragm suddenly tightening so that you take a short gasp of air. The "hic" is the sound made by your vocal cords snapping shut.

Breathing problems

There are many different reasons why people have breathing problems. People with asthma have very delicate bronchioles which sometimes close up and stop them from breathing out. Asthma sufferers use an inhaler to blow medicine into their bronchioles to keep them open.

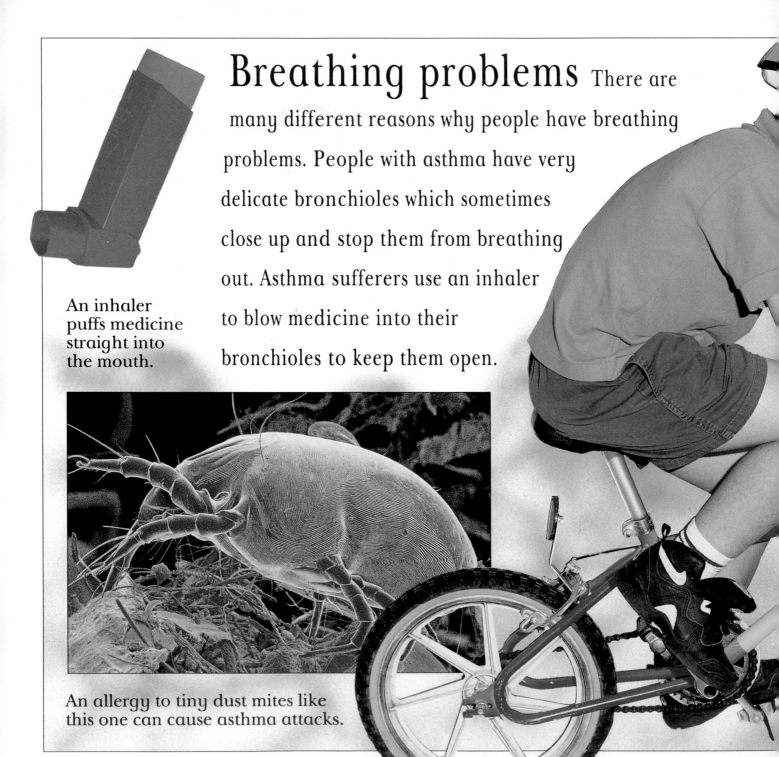

An inhaler puffs medicine straight into the mouth.

An allergy to tiny dust mites like this one can cause asthma attacks.

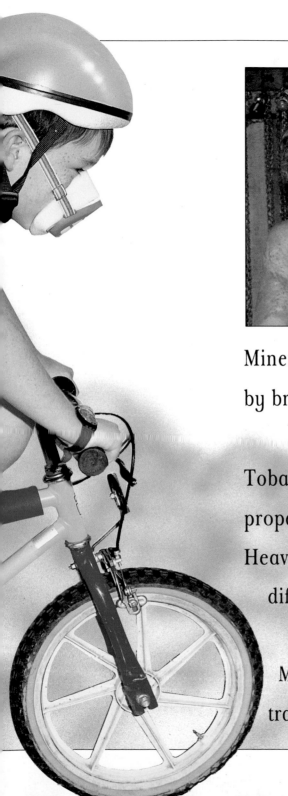

Miners sometimes suffer from chest complaints caused by breathing in dusty air every day.

Tobacco smoke stops a smoker's cilia from working properly so that mucus and dirt build up in the lungs. Heavy smokers often develop bad coughs and find it difficult to breathe easily.

Many cyclists now wear masks to help prevent traffic exhaust from damaging their lungs.

Chapter Five
Eating

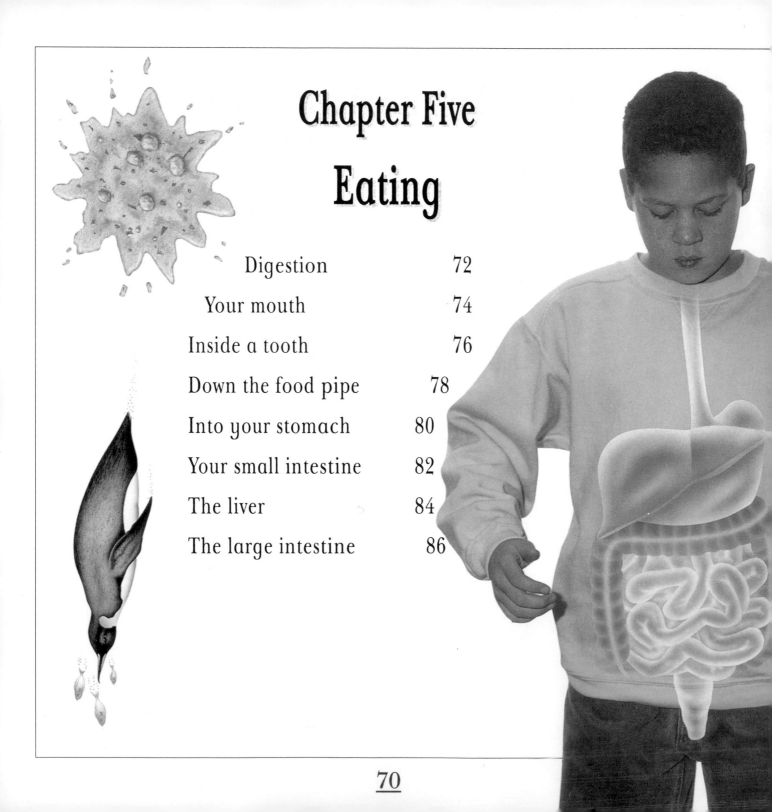

Digestion 72

Your mouth 74

Inside a tooth 76

Down the food pipe 78

Into your stomach 80

Your small intestine 82

The liver 84

The large intestine 86

Introduction

From the moment you put food into your mouth you start to break it down into something your body can use. This process is called digestion, and its purpose is to extract as many nutrients as possible from your food. These are then used by the body to produce energy, build new body parts, or repair those that are damaged.

All of this is dependent on the quality of food you eat. Poor food may mean that your body will not get all the nutrients it needs, and you could become ill.

Digestion

Digestion starts as soon as you put food in your mouth. It carries on for about 20 hours as the food travels through your digestive system. This is a series of tunnels and caves inside your body. These are all different sizes, shapes, and lengths.

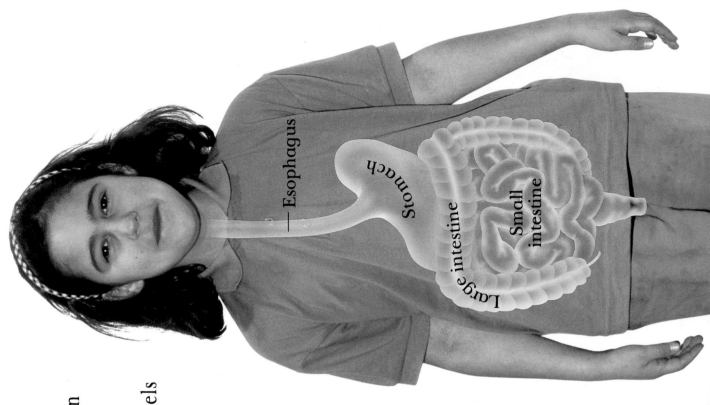

Esophagus

Stomach

Large intestine

Small intestine

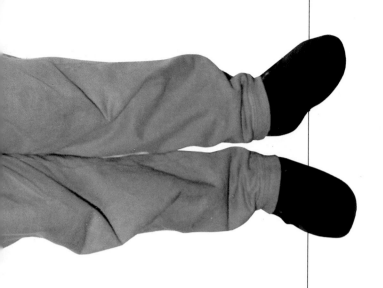

If they were laid in a straight line, they would stretch more than 26 feet (eight meters) – the average width of a swimming pool!

Your body digests food slowly by breaking it down into smaller pieces, separating it into useful parts – nutrients and waste matter. Food is completely digested when it has passed from your digestive system into your blood. Your blood then carries the nutrients around your body.

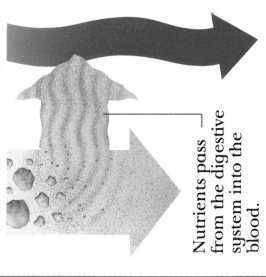

Food is broken down in the digestive system.

Nutrients pass from the digestive system into the blood.

Your mouth

Each part of your mouth has a special job to do. If you eat an apple, you bite into it with your front teeth. The four teeth in the middle of your top and bottom jaws, the incisors, are used for cutting and chopping. The sharp, fanglike teeth on either side of your incisors are used for cutting and tearing. These are your canine teeth.

Your tongue pushes the apple back to your molars for chewing.

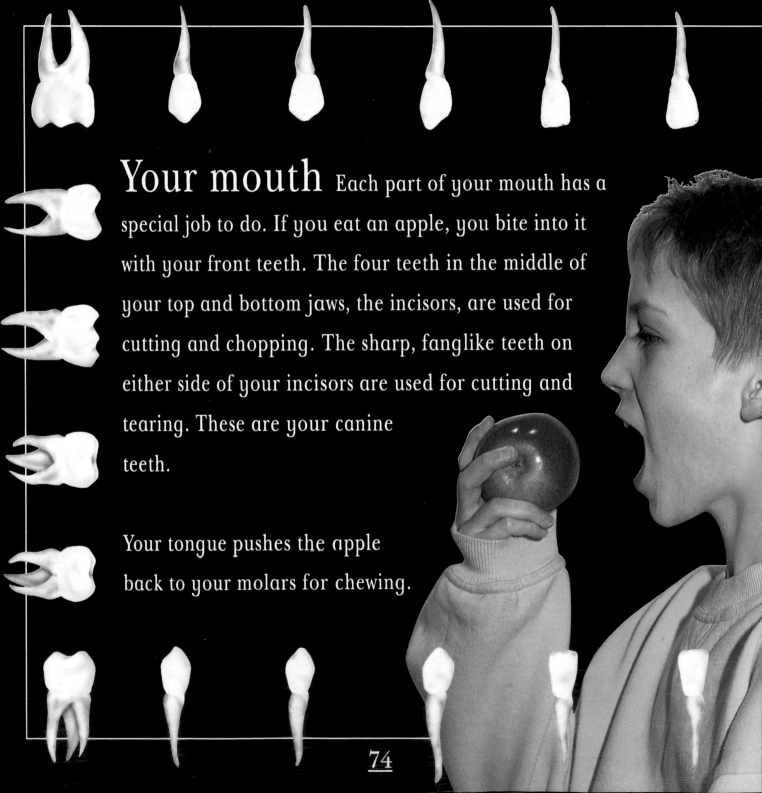

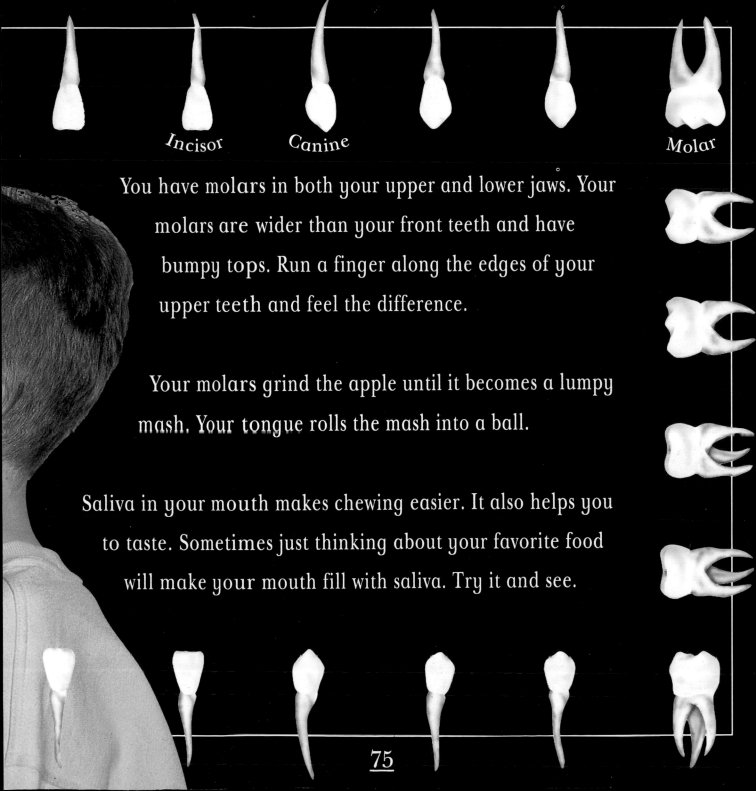

Incisor Canine Molar

You have molars in both your upper and lower jaws. Your molars are wider than your front teeth and have bumpy tops. Run a finger along the edges of your upper teeth and feel the difference.

Your molars grind the apple until it becomes a lumpy mash. Your tongue rolls the mash into a ball.

Saliva in your mouth makes chewing easier. It also helps you to taste. Sometimes just thinking about your favorite food will make your mouth fill with saliva. Try it and see.

Inside a tooth

When you look into your mouth, you see only the top half of each tooth. This part is called the crown. It is covered in tough, white enamel. Enamel is the hardest material in your body.

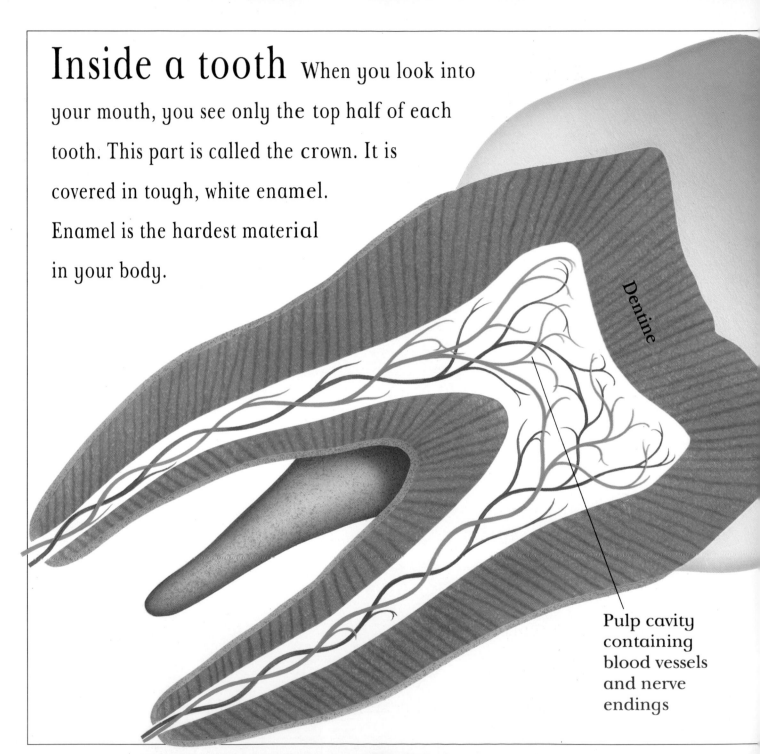

Dentine

Pulp cavity containing blood vessels and nerve endings

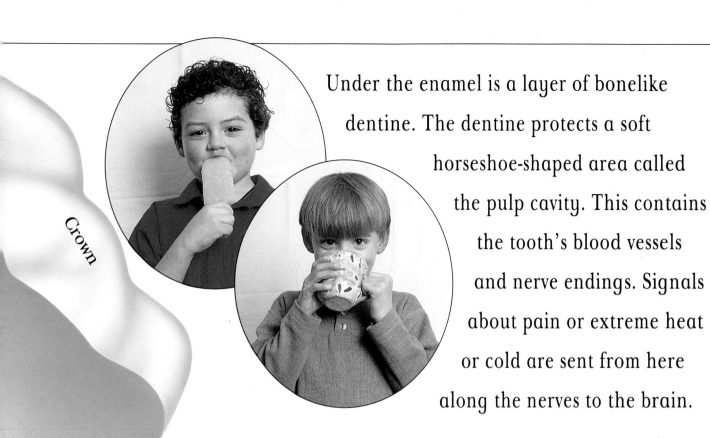

Crown

Under the enamel is a layer of bonelike dentine. The dentine protects a soft horseshoe-shaped area called the pulp cavity. This contains the tooth's blood vessels and nerve endings. Signals about pain or extreme heat or cold are sent from here along the nerves to the brain.

The dentine and pulp cavity reach down into the root of the tooth. Front teeth have just one root, while some back teeth have two or three roots. The root is attached firmly into the jaw bone by a kind of bony glue called cement.

Gum

Jaw bone

Roots

Down the food pipe
Your tongue pushes the ball of mash into your food pipe. This is called your esophagus. As you swallow, a flap (your epiglottis) drops over your windpipe. This stops food from going down the wrong way.

Sometimes your epiglottis does not drop down in time. When this happens, you have to cough hard until the food is blown out of your windpipe.

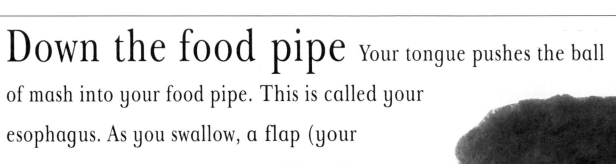

Esophagus

Food mash

Your esophagus is a stretchy tube about ten inches (25 centimeters) long. Its walls are made of muscles which squeeze food downward. They do this without you thinking about it. To see how they work, put a tennis ball down a long sock. Like the muscles in your esophagus, you have to squeeze your hands hard together just behind the ball to move it along.

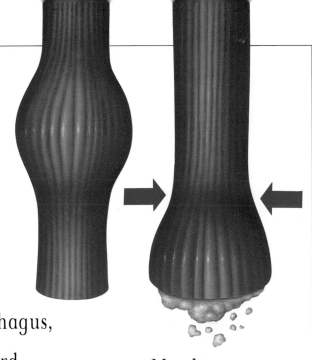

Muscles squeeze behind the food to push it down.

Because food is squeezed along your esophagus, and does not simply fall down it, it is possible to eat in almost any position – even standing on your head! This means that astronauts can enjoy a meal even when floating around their cabin! (But remember, it is safest to eat when you are upright.)

Into your stomach

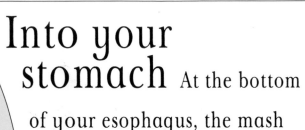

Rib cage

Stomach

At the bottom of your esophagus, the mash passes into your stomach. This is a stretchy bag shaped like a boxing glove. It lies just below your ribs. Food stays here for three to five hours.

During this time, your stomach churns the mash with gastric juices from your stomach wall. These juices kill any germs in the mash and help to break the food down into smaller parts. When the mash has turned into a kind of thick soup, it is ready to leave your stomach.

Gate of muscle

Food soup

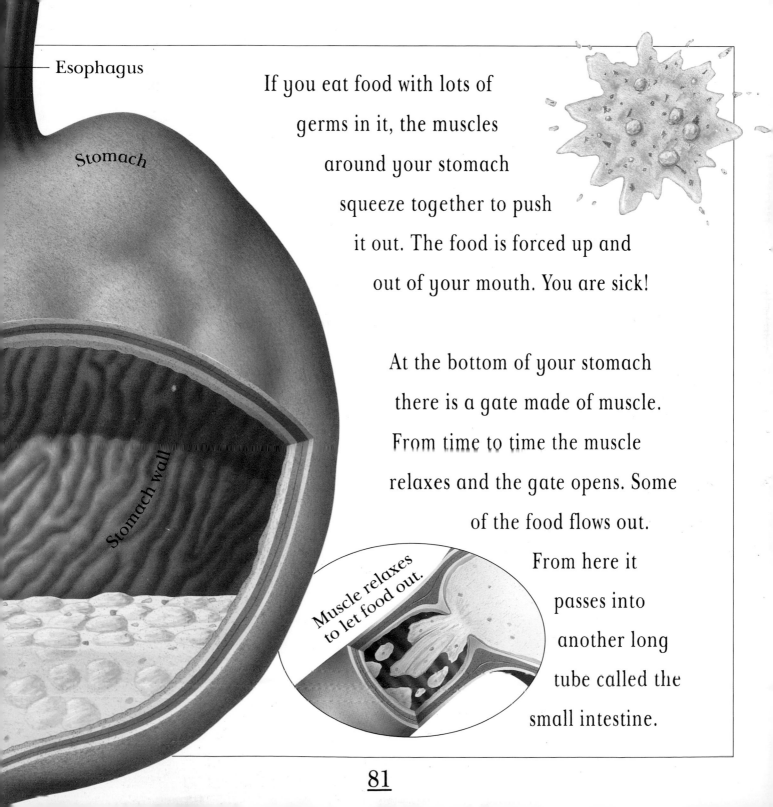

Esophagus

Stomach

Stomach wall

Muscle relaxes to let food out.

If you eat food with lots of germs in it, the muscles around your stomach squeeze together to push it out. The food is forced up and out of your mouth. You are sick!

At the bottom of your stomach there is a gate made of muscle. From time to time the muscle relaxes and the gate opens. Some of the food flows out. From here it passes into another long tube called the small intestine.

Your small intestine

Your small intestine is about 23 feet (seven meters) long. That's as long as five seven-year-olds laid head to toe! It can take up to four hours for the food to travel from one end to the other.

In the first part of the small intestine, food is mixed with juices from your pancreas and bile from your liver which help to break it down even further.

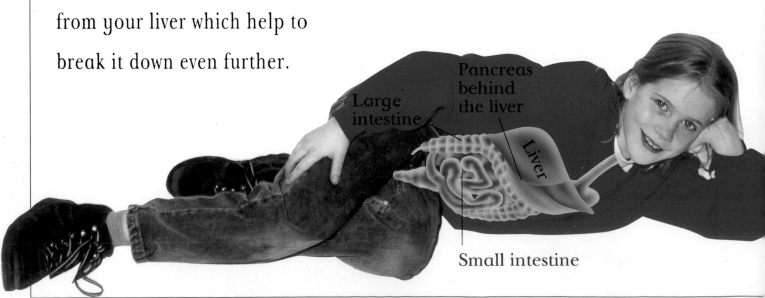

Large intestine

Pancreas behind the liver

Liver

Small intestine

It is then squeezed on through your intestine, becoming more and more watery as it goes.

As the almost-liquid food reaches the end of your small intestine, nutrients pass through its walls into your blood. The walls are lined with thousands of tiny "fingers," called villi, to help absorb the nutrients more quickly.

Your blood carries most of the nutrients to your liver. Undigested food then travels to your large intestine.

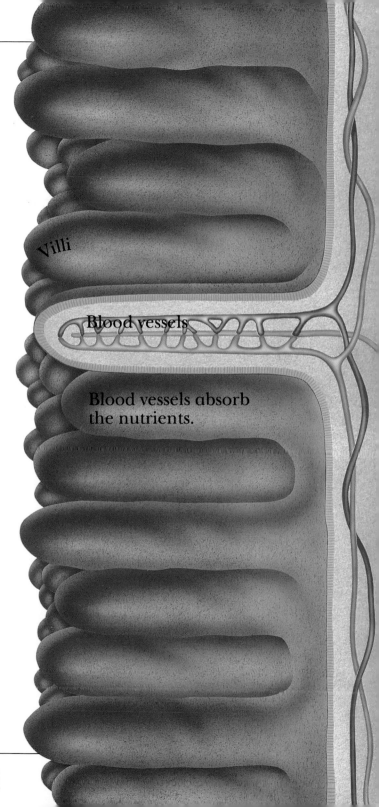

Villi

Blood vessels

Blood vessels absorb the nutrients.

The liver

Your liver lies mostly on your right side, protected by your lower ribs. It weighs between two and four pounds (one and two kilograms.) That's about the same weight as your brain.

Before any food can be used by your body, it has to be cleaned and prepared by your liver. Your liver filters the nutrients and blood to take out any leftover waste. It turns some of the waste into bile which travels through the bile duct and out of the liver.

Liver

Liver

Gall bladder

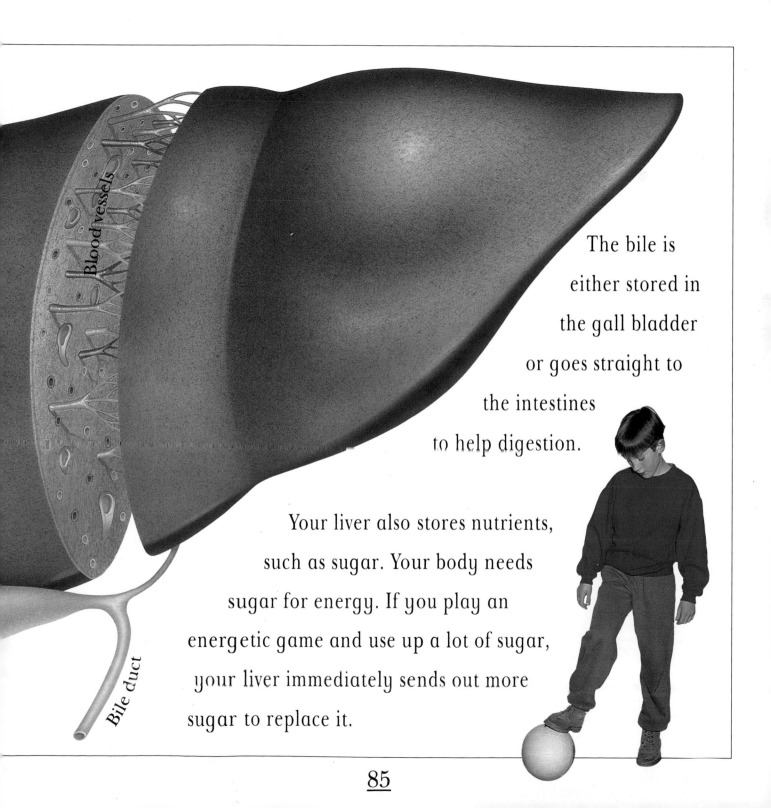

Blood vessels

Bile duct

The bile is either stored in the gall bladder or goes straight to the intestines to help digestion.

Your liver also stores nutrients, such as sugar. Your body needs sugar for energy. If you play an energetic game and use up a lot of sugar, your liver immediately sends out more sugar to replace it.

The large intestine

Your large intestine carries undigested food and water from your small intestine to your rectum.

Your large intestine is wider than your small intestine, but only half as long. It takes up to 24 hours for the contents to complete the journey from beginning to end.

As food and water travel along, a lot of water is sucked through the wall of your large intestine into your blood. Then only waste food is left. Slowly it gets harder. By the time it reaches your rectum, it is quite solid. This solid waste, called feces, is stored in your rectum until you are ready to push it out through your anus when you go to the bathroom.

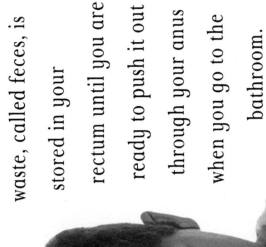

Esophagus

Large intestine

Small intestine

Rectum

Chapter Six

Senses

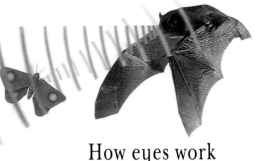

How eyes work   90

Working together   92

Eye problems   93

How ears work   94

Balance   96

Smell   98

Taste   100

Touch   102

Introduction

Every moment of the day, you are bombarded with a
stream of information from the world around you.
These bits of information come in the form of things
you see, smell, hear, taste, and touch. They are
received by sensors in the eyes, nose, ears, tongue, and
skin. These convert the information into signals that are
passed to the brain along the nervous system.

Together, these pieces of information help
you interact with the outside world, as well
as with each other.

How eyes work

Behind each pupil is a lens. This is like a small, curved piece of jelly. As light enters your eye, the lens bends it to form a tiny upside down picture of what you see on the retina at the back of your eye.

Your retina is made up of millions of tiny nerve endings. It sends messages along the optic nerve to your brain. The

brain sorts out the messages. It turns the picture right side up, and decides what color and size everything is.

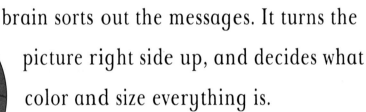

Close-up of the retina, showing blind spot (in yellow)

Part of your retina, your blind spot, is not sensitive to light. Look at the two pictures below. Cover your left eye and look at the apple. Slowly move the book toward you. When the carrot vanishes, you have found your blind spot.

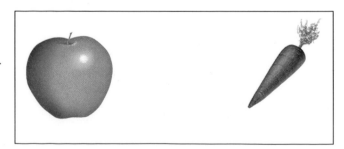

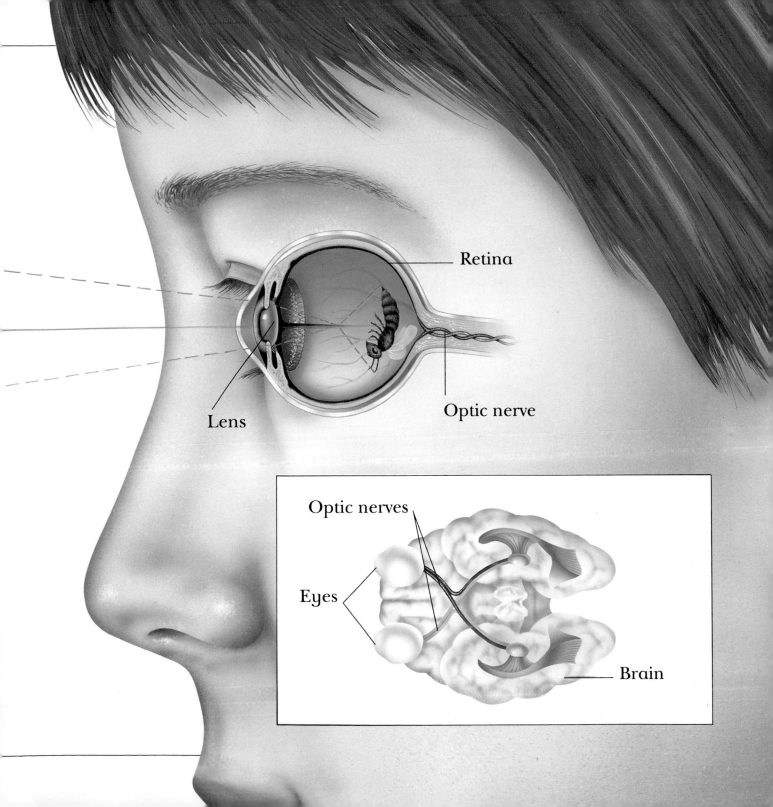

Retina

Lens

Optic nerve

Optic nerves

Eyes

Brain

Working together

Normally you do not notice your blind spot. If one eye cannot see something, the other usually can.

Hold up a pen and close your left eye. Line up the pen with a clock on the wall. Now open your left eye and close your right without moving the pen. What happens?

The pen has moved because each of your eyes sees it from a different angle.

Eye problems

Many people are nearsighted or farsighted. This means that the picture formed at the back of their eye falls just in front of the retina, or just behind it. Glasses or contact lenses help them to see clearly.

Farsight

Nearsight

A few people are colorblind. This usually means that they cannot tell red from green. Look at this circle of dots. Can you see a number in it?

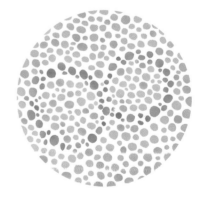

How ears work

Your ears – the parts you can see – funnel sound waves into your ear canals and on to your eardrums.

Your eardrum is a thin piece of skin stretched across the end of your ear canal. When sound waves touch your eardrum, it vibrates. The vibrations pass from your eardrum to three small bones: the hammer, anvil, and stirrup.

From here the vibrations flow to a coiled tube called the cochlea. It contains thousands of hair-like nerve endings and is filled with liquid. When the liquid vibrates, the hairs move. These change the vibrations into messages. The messages are sent to your brain, which decides what they mean.

Wax duct

Ear canal

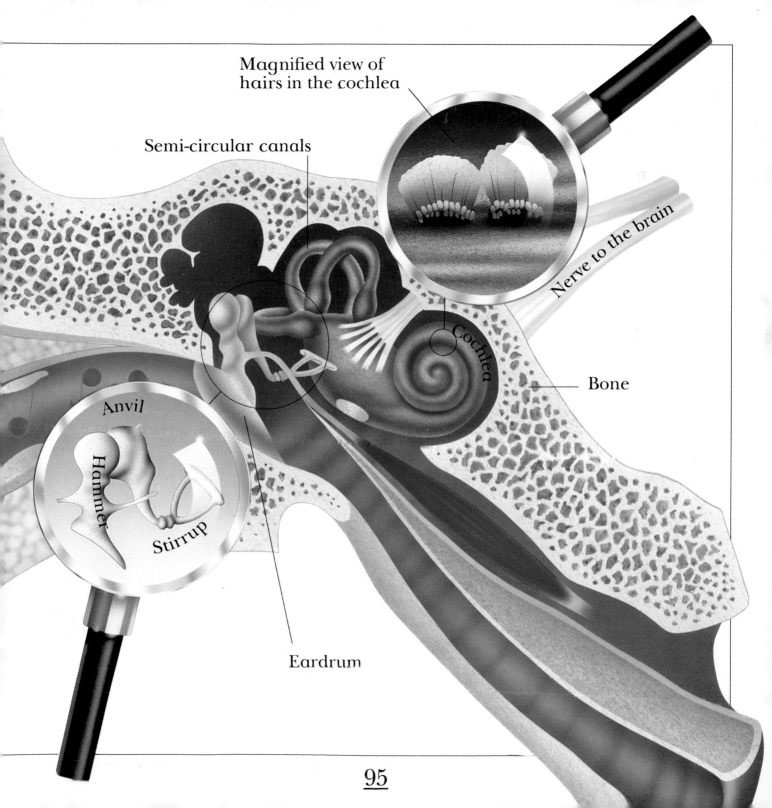

Magnified view of
hairs in the cochlea

Semi-circular canals

Nerve to the brain

Cochlea

Bone

Anvil

Hammer

Stirrup

Eardrum

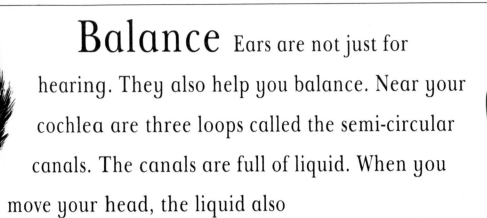

Balance

Ears are not just for hearing. They also help you balance. Near your cochlea are three loops called the semi-circular canals. The canals are full of liquid. When you move your head, the liquid also moves. It pushes against hairlike nerve endings, which send messages to your brain. From these messages your brain can work out what position your head is in.

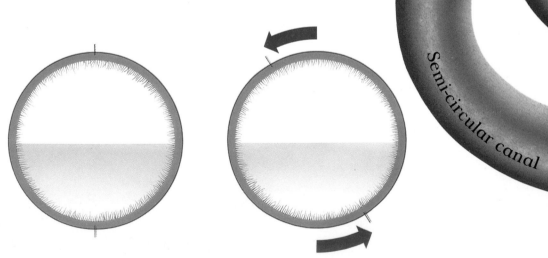

Semi-circular canal

Liquid in the canals moves as you move your head.

Pour a few drops of water into a glass jar. Move the jar quickly around so that the water swirls up the sides. Now stop the jar. What happens to the water?

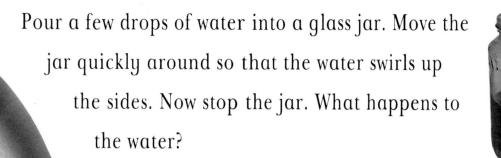

Nerves to brain

The same thing happens if you spin around too fast. When you stop, the liquid in your semi-circular canals keeps moving. The nerve endings go on sending messages to your brain. Meanwhile your eyes tell you that you are standing still. Your brain gets muddled and you feel dizzy.

Smell

How many smells can you think of? Which do you like? Which do you dislike? Believe it or not, your brain can pick out over 10,000 different smells!

When you breathe in, air travels up your nose and into a space called the nasal cavity. The cavity roof is packed with millions of tiny hairs. They are rooted in a thick, sticky liquid called mucus – like reeds in a pond. Scent particles in the air mix with the mucus and are caught by the hairs. Nerve endings in the hairs send messages to your brain, and your brain decides what the scent is.

Some smells make you feel happy, others sad. Some make you feel hungry. Others make you feel sick. Smells can warn you not to eat bad food, or tell you that something is burning.

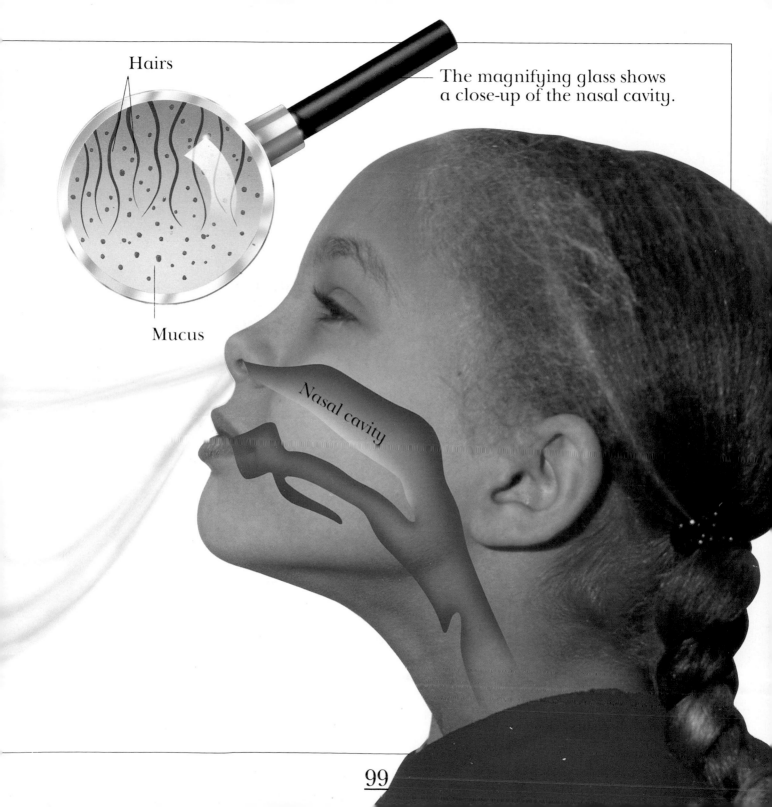

Hairs

Mucus

The magnifying glass shows
a close-up of the nasal cavity.

Nasal cavity

Taste

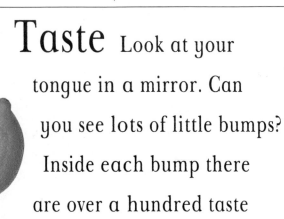

Look at your tongue in a mirror. Can you see lots of little bumps? Inside each bump there are over a hundred taste buds which pick up the different tastes in your food.

You have different taste buds to pick up each type of taste – salty, sweet, sour, and bitter. You can find out where they are on your tongue. Use Q-Tips to dab bits of salt, sugar, lemon juice (sour), and coffee grounds (bitter) on your tongue. Where does each taste seem strongest?

Bitter

Not many taste buds

Sour

Sweet and salty

Now dry your tongue with a piece of paper towel. Put some sugar on the tip. How long is it before you taste the sugar? You can only taste food when it is mixed with saliva.

It is easier to taste food if you can smell it, too. Try eating pieces of peeled apple and peeled potato while holding your nose. Can you tell which is which? Have you noticed that food doesn't taste as good when you have a cold-blocked nose?

Touch

The skin that covers your body is full of tiny nerve endings which give you information about things that are in contact with your body.

Shut your eyes and pick fruits from a bowl. Feel each fruit in turn. Can you recognize each one? What makes them different?

Nerve endings in your skin can tell if something is hot or cold, rough or smooth. They can also feel something pressing against you, or hurting you. You have at least 20 types of nerve endings which send all kinds of messages to your brain.

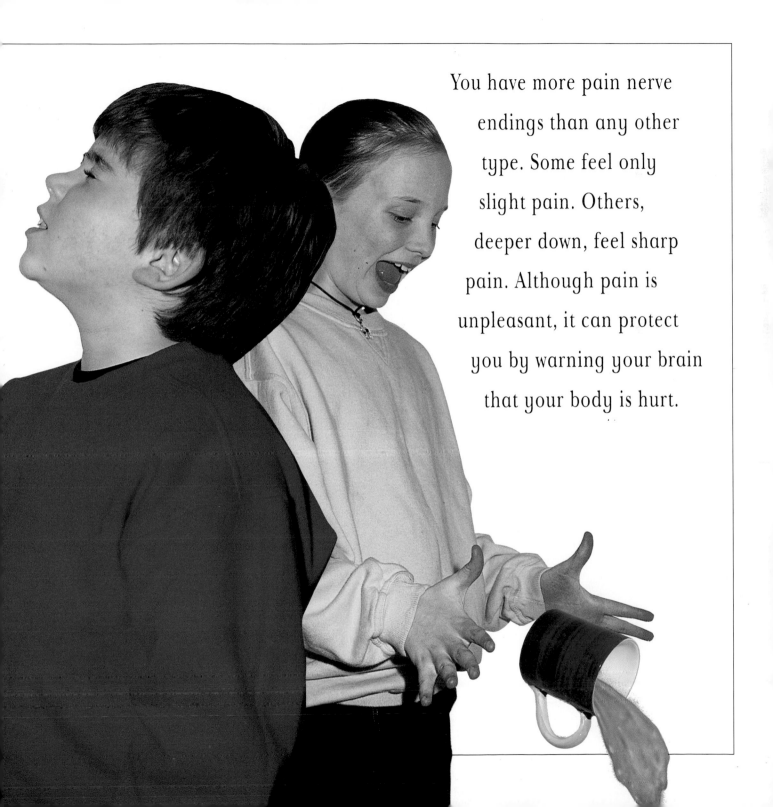

You have more pain nerve endings than any other type. Some feel only slight pain. Others, deeper down, feel sharp pain. Although pain is unpleasant, it can protect you by warning your brain that your body is hurt.

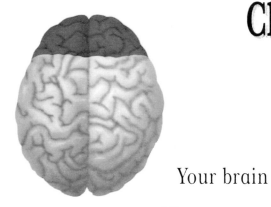

Chapter Seven
Brain

Your brain — 106

The nervous system — 108

Nerve signals — 110

The cerebrum — 112

Learning — 114

Memory — 116

Sleep — 118

The cerebellum — 120

The brain stem — 121

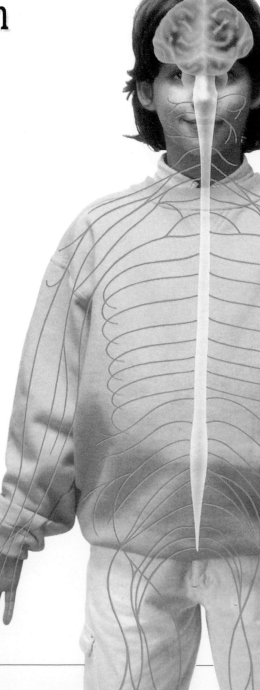

Introduction

Welcome to the part of your body that runs the whole show – the brain. This collection of millions of nerve cells controls everything from the way you walk and how you breathe, to the more subconscious things, such as your dreams.

Connecting this incredibly powerful computer is a network of tiny fibers, called nerves. These carry messages to all parts of the body, sending information to the brain as well as carrying back any commands the brain chooses to make.

Your brain

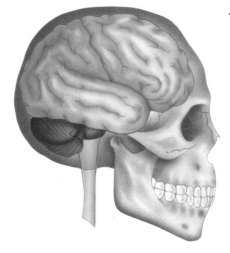

Your brain fills the upper half of your head. It is like a soft, pinkish-gray wrinkled sponge. More than three quarters of it is made of water. Without a skull to support and protect your brain, it would sag like jelly.

The brain is made up of three main parts. The largest of these, the cerebrum, is divided into two walnut-shaped halves. The cerebrum is the thinking part of the brain. It allows you to move how you want, to solve problems, and to remember.

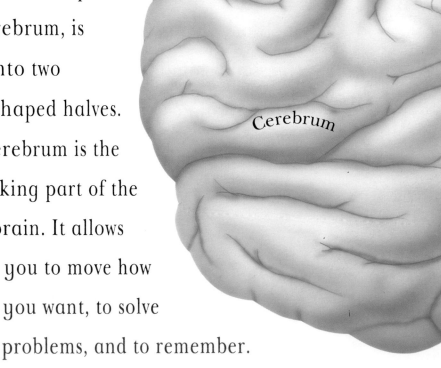

Cerebrum

Cerebrum

Cerebellum

Brain stem

Below the cerebrum, at the back of the brain, is the cerebellum. This makes sure your body muscles work together smoothly. It also helps you to keep your balance. The brain stem helps to control how your body machine works. Among other things, it is partly responsible for your heartbeat, your breathing, and the digestion of your food.

The nervous system

Together the three areas of your brain control how your body works by receiving and sending signals to different parts of it. The signals travel along bundles of fine, hairlike threads called nerves.

Some signals travel straight to the brain. Most pass first through the spinal cord – a long bundle of nerves inside your backbone, or spine. Like your brain, your spinal cord is more than three-quarters water.

Brain

Nerve

Spinal cord

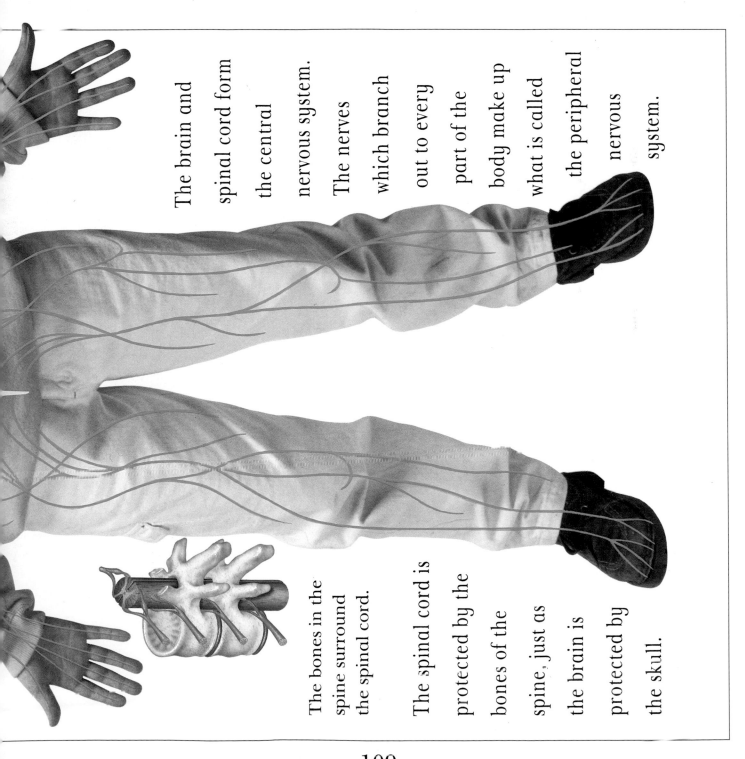

The brain and spinal cord form the central nervous system. The nerves which branch out to every part of the body make up what is called the peripheral nervous system.

The bones in the spine surround the spinal cord.

The spinal cord is protected by the bones of the spine, just as the brain is protected by the skull.

Nerve signals

A wasp is about to land on your hand. What do you do?

First your eyes send a warning signal to your brain. Your brain immediately sends another signal back to your muscles, telling them to move your hand. Your brain decides exactly how your hand should move.

Movements like these are called voluntary movements.

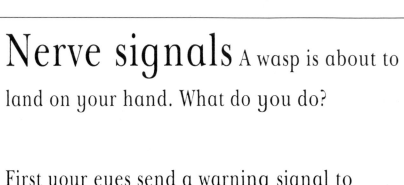

The green arrows show the direction of the nerve signals.

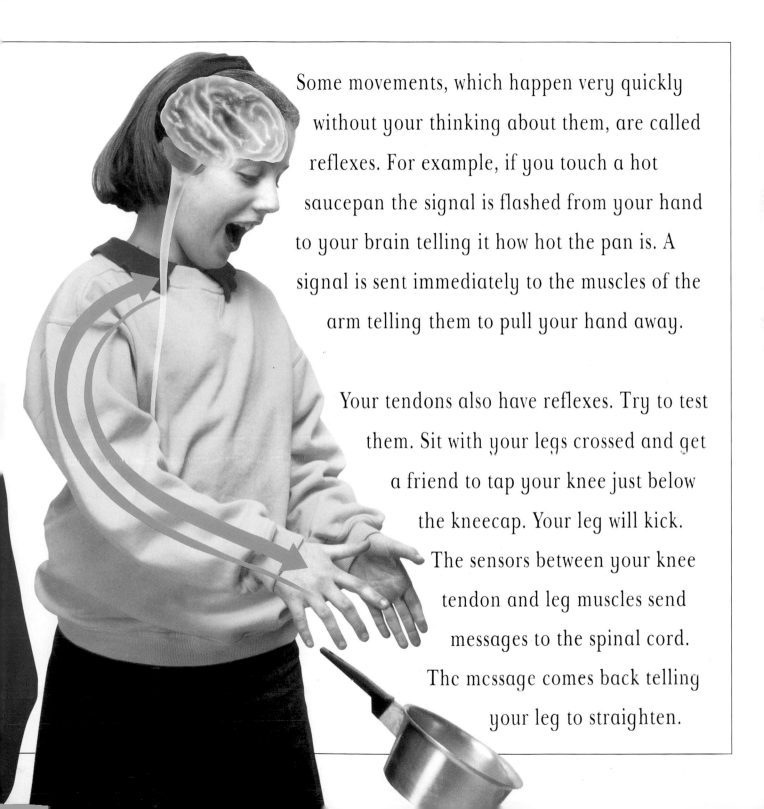

Some movements, which happen very quickly without your thinking about them, are called reflexes. For example, if you touch a hot saucepan the signal is flashed from your hand to your brain telling it how hot the pan is. A signal is sent immediately to the muscles of the arm telling them to pull your hand away.

Your tendons also have reflexes. Try to test them. Sit with your legs crossed and get a friend to tap your knee just below the kneecap. Your leg will kick. The sensors between your knee tendon and leg muscles send messages to the spinal cord. The message comes back telling your leg to straighten.

The cerebrum

Most of the muscles that move your head, body, and limbs work only when you want them to. They are called voluntary muscles. They are controlled by the cortex, the outer layer of the cerebrum.

Unlike animals, humans have a wrinkled cortex with deep folds. If it were unfolded, the cortex would cover an area 30 times as big. The cortex is divided into many areas which receive and transmit different signals.

The voluntary muscles are controlled by an area running across the two halves of the cerebrum. This is called the motor area.

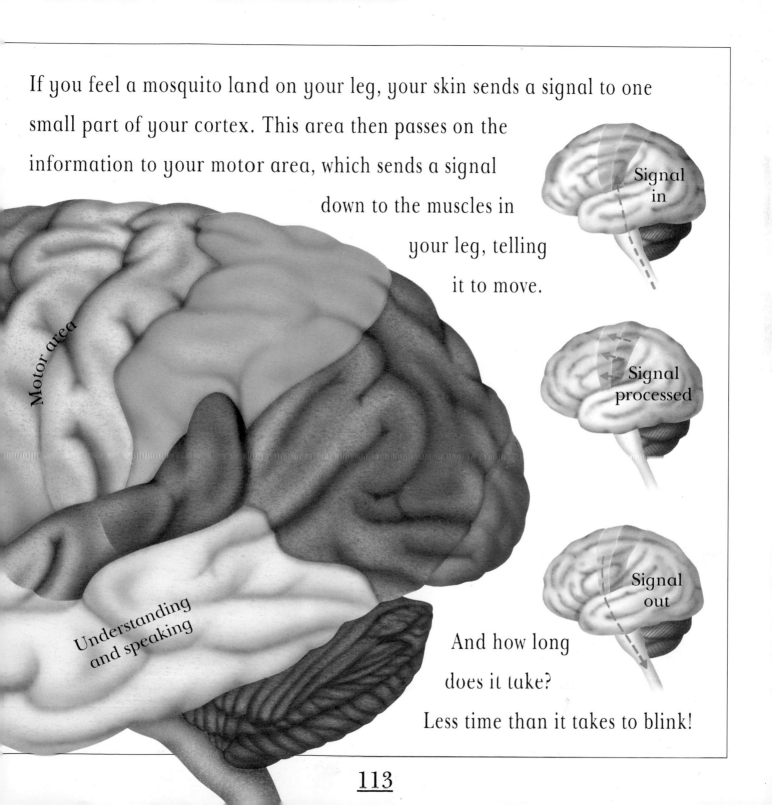

If you feel a mosquito land on your leg, your skin sends a signal to one small part of your cortex. This area then passes on the information to your motor area, which sends a signal down to the muscles in your leg, telling it to move.

Signal in

Signal processed

Signal out

Motor area

Understanding and speaking

And how long does it take? Less time than it takes to blink!

Learning

How do you learn?
Like other parts of your body, most of your
nervous system is made up of millions of tiny
cells. These cells are called neurons. All neurons
have a body. Each has a long "tail," or nerve fiber,
linking it to other neurons, muscles, or
other parts of your body. Some nerve fibers
are less than an inch long. Others can stretch up to
three feet (1m) – from your spinal cord to your big toe!

Each neuron also has lots of branches sprouting
from its center. Nerve fibers from other
neurons are attached to these
branches. This means that every
neuron is linked to thousands of
other neurons.

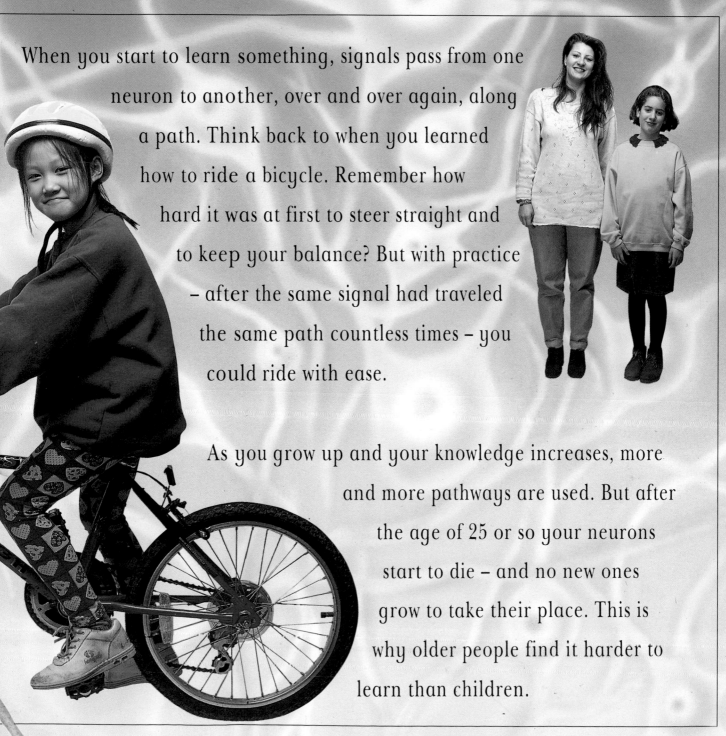

When you start to learn something, signals pass from one neuron to another, over and over again, along a path. Think back to when you learned how to ride a bicycle. Remember how hard it was at first to steer straight and to keep your balance? But with practice – after the same signal had traveled the same path countless times – you could ride with ease.

As you grow up and your knowledge increases, more and more pathways are used. But after the age of 25 or so your neurons start to die – and no new ones grow to take their place. This is why older people find it harder to learn than children.

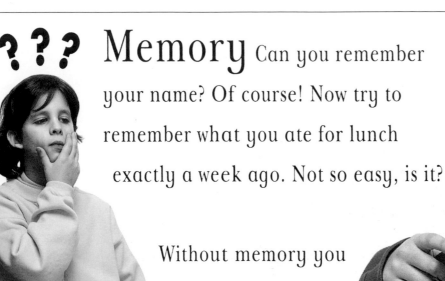

??? Memory

Can you remember your name? Of course! Now try to remember what you ate for lunch exactly a week ago. Not so easy, is it?

Without memory you could not learn anything. It is thought that there are two types of memory – a long-term memory and a short-term memory.

Things that you learn early are kept in your long-term memory. These include facts (such as your name and address), actions (for example, how to brush your teeth), and even sights, sounds, smells, and tastes. Strong feelings, too, are kept in your long-term memory.

You use your short-term memory to store things which happened a few minutes or hours ago.

Try playing the shopping game. Start by saying, "I'm going shopping to buy some bread." The next person continues, "I'm going shopping to buy some bread and some apples," and so on.

How long is the list before somebody forgets something?

Many older people find it hard to remember things which happened a short time ago. Yet they can often remember events which took place when they were young. See if your grandparents can remember their first day of school. Can you?

I'm going shopping to buy some bread and...

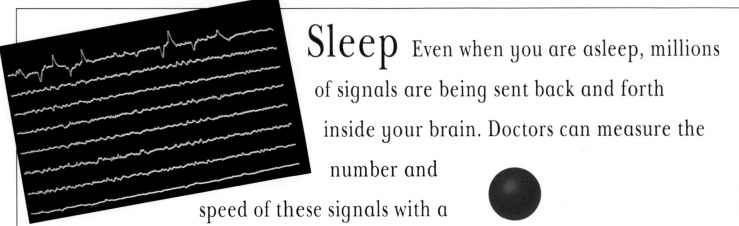

Sleep

Even when you are asleep, millions of signals are being sent back and forth inside your brain. Doctors can measure the number and speed of these signals with a special machine. The machine displays the signals as patterns of wavy lines (sometimes called brain waves). This display is called an EEG. Doctors use EEGs to help them find out what is wrong with a patient's brain.

The wave patterns change as your brain becomes more or less active. When you are awake and thinking hard, the waves are small and spiky.

When you are relaxed (while you are watching television, for example), the waves are taller and wider.

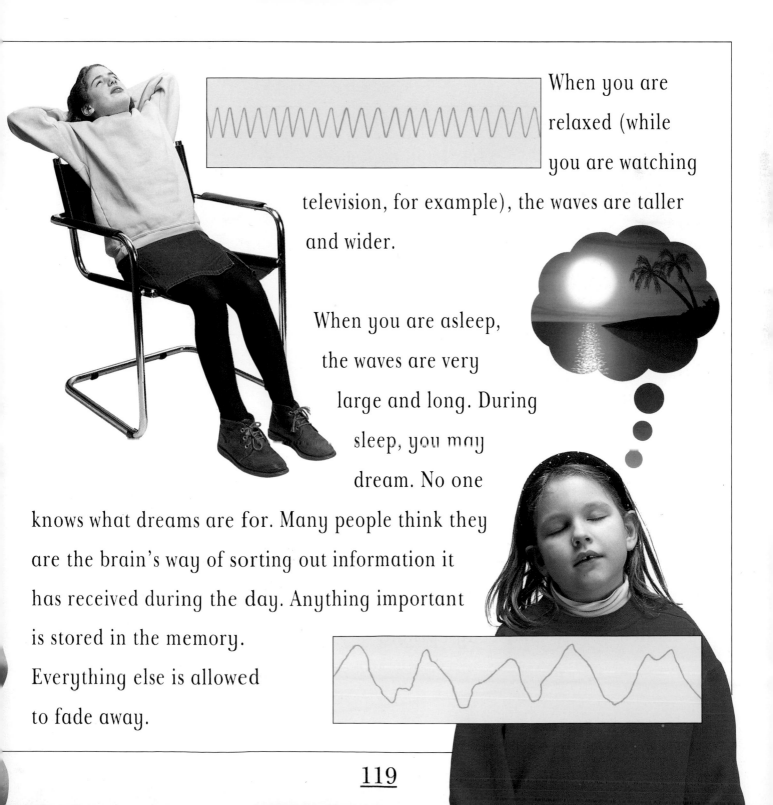

When you are asleep, the waves are very large and long. During sleep, you may dream. No one knows what dreams are for. Many people think they are the brain's way of sorting out information it has received during the day. Anything important is stored in the memory. Everything else is allowed to fade away.

The cerebellum

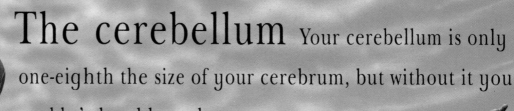

Your cerebellum is only one-eighth the size of your cerebrum, but without it you wouldn't be able to do any but the simplest movements. You couldn't even pat your head, or rub your tummy.

Your cerebellum also helps you to keep your balance and to stand up straight. Without a cerebellum, tightrope walking would be impossible!

Next time you are standing on a bus or train, notice how your legs automatically bend and straighten to keep your body upright.

The brain stem

Your brain stem attaches your brain to your spinal cord. It helps to control muscles in your body over which your mind has no power. If you are exercising, it tells your lungs to breathe more deeply; if you have just eaten breakfast, it tells your stomach to start digesting.

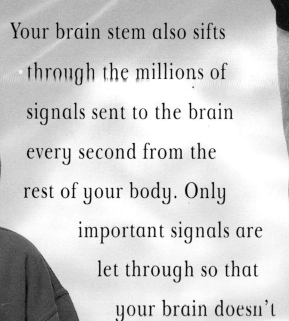

Your brain stem also sifts through the millions of signals sent to the brain every second from the rest of your body. Only important signals are let through so that your brain doesn't get confused.

DID YOU KNOW?

... that your fingerprints took shape while you were growing in your mommy's tummy? They are different from everyone else's in the world.

... that you have the same number of bones in your neck as a giraffe – seven?

... that your heart pumps over one gallon (half a bucketful) of blood a minute around your body?

... that pearl divers in the Pacific Ocean can hold their breath for between two and three minutes? **DO NOT TRY THIS YOURSELF!**

... that a newborn baby sees the world upside down? It takes some time before the baby's brain learns to turn the picture right side up.

... that nerve messages travel at very different speeds? They vary between one and a half feet to 400 feet per second – faster than a high-speed train.

... that every day the salivary glands in your mouth will produce about one half-gallon of saliva?

Glossary

Alveolus – One of many bubble-shaped air sacs found in the lungs, found at the end of the bronchi.

Artery – A vessel that carries blood under great pressure from the heart around the body.

Bronchus – A branch of the windpipe, that enters the lungs and branches into smaller tubes, which end with the alveoli.

Cartilage – A type of body tissue that supports joints and helps them move smoothly.

Cerebellum – The part of the brain, found at the top of the spine, that aids balance and helps your muscles work together.

Cerebrum – The largest part of the brain, it controls your movements and receives signals.

Cochlea – The coiled tube in the ear which detects the vibrations made by noises.

Dermis – The bottom layer of your skin, which contains nerve endings, hair roots, and sweat glands.

Epidermis – The upper layer of skin, where new skin cells are formed.

Esophagus – The pipe which carries food and liquid down into your stomach.

Follicle – A small tube of skin containing the hair root.

Heart – The organ that pumps your blood around your body.

Joint – The place where two bones meet.

Marrow – A fatty jelly found inside many bones. Red bone marrow is responsible for making all the blood cells.

Nerve – A fine thread that carries information around the body.

Nervous system – The collective name for the brain, spinal cord, and nerves.

Plasma – The liquid part of blood.

Pulse – The beating of the heart and the arteries that you can feel.

Spinal cord – A long bundle of nerves inside your backbone.

Vein – A vessel that carries blood back to your heart from the body.

Villus – A tiny finger-like projection which speeds up the rate of absorption. These are found in places such as the intestine.

Index

adam's apple 64

alveoli 59, 124

arms 18, 28-29, 30

arteries 41, 48, 49, 50,
 124

asthma 68

bones 122

 compact 20, 21

 marrow 20, 21, 125

 spongy 21

blood 21, 42-43, 49, 50,
73, 83, 84, 86, 122, 124

clots 44

 plasma 41, 42, 125

brain 26, 52, 84, 88,
 91, 94, 95, 96, 124

 motor area 112

 stem 107, 121

bronchi 58, 59, 61,
 124

capillaries 49, 50

carbon dioxide 42, 62

cartilage 22, 24, 28,
 124

cerebellum 107, 120,
 124

cerebrum 112, 124

chest 54, 56, 60, 62

cochlea 94, 96, 124

diaphragm 56, 60, 61,
 62, 67

digestive system 53,
 72, 81, 82, 83, 86, 87

ears 27, 94-97

epiglottis 78

esophagus 78, 79, 80, 87, 125

eyes 27, 90-93, 97

   lens 90, 91

face 27

fingers 28

follicle, hair 14, 15, 16, 125

fractures, bone 34

gallbladder 85

germs 36, 38, 43, 44, 80, 81

hair 4, 10, 11, 12-17,

67

hands 28, 60

head 4, 12, 18

heart 41, 46-47, 50, 52, 56, 58, 122, 125

hiccups 67

joints 18, 32-33, 125

kidneys 41

knees 30, 31

legs 18, 30

ligaments 33

lips 12, 65

liver 53, 82, 83, 84-85

lungs 42, 46, 47, 54,

56-59, 67, 124

melanin 7

memory 116-117

mouth 53, 61, 74-75

mucus 66, 67, 98

muscle 50, 52, 56, 79, 81

nasal cavity 98, 99

nerves 9, 10, 90, 91, 95, 97, 98 108, 109, 110, 111, 123, 125

neurons 114, 115

nose 58, 61

pancreas 82

Index

pupil 90

reflexes 111

retina 90, 91, 93

saliva 75, 101, 123

skin 4, 6-11, 18, 36, 50, 101

skull 23, 26-27, 32, 106

sleep 118-119

smell 98, 99

sneeze 66

spine 24-25, 30, 108, 109

stomach 72, 80-81, 87

sweat glands 10, 11

talking 64-65

taste 75, 100-101

teeth 27, 65, 74, 76, 77

tendons 111

tongue 65, 74, 78, 100

veins 41, 48, 50-51, 125

windpipe 56, 61, 64, 78, 124

Photo Credits

Associated British Pictures Co. (courtesy Kobal Collection), Bruce Coleman, Eye Ubiquitous, Frank Spooner Pictures, Mary Evans Picture Library, Paul Nightingale, Roger Vlitos, Science Photo Library, Spectrum Colour Library